How to Be a Good Boyfriend

34 ways to keep her from getting annoying, jealous, or crazy

by Rebecca A. Marquis

How to Be a Good Boyfriend: 34 ways to keep her from getting annoying, jealous, or crazy
By Rebecca A. Marquis

ISBN 1-456-32411-X
ISBN 978-1-456-32411-7

Email: rebecca.a.marquis@gmail.com

To Debbie, Dina, and Ann
for turning my tears into laughter and wisdom

Contents

Introduction

<u>To the guys</u>: I know what you're looking for. You want a woman in your life who is fun to hang out with (including a fun sex life), who is a supportive friend, and who isn't annoying or crazy. I get it. But what you probably don't realize is that the little things you do can turn us into the annoying, jealous, crazy girlfriend. We need three things from you. Give us these three things and it'll be the best relationship you've ever had. Don't, and we'll get annoying. We'll get jealous. We might even get a little crazy. If you want to have a great time with her without the drama or the headaches, keep reading. This book is for you.

<u>To the ladies</u>: Work with me here. Although this book is written as a how-to guide for guys, we have to do our part too. Throughout the book there are *"A Note to the Ladies"* sections. Please read them. Understand them. They will save your relationship.

What's written in this book is not based on any scientific research, interviews with experts, or mass surveys. This is simply what my friends and I have been talking about for years. Take from it what you like. The women I'm writing about are mature, successful, sane women who are interested in having a good relationship. The stories are based on true events, although names, identifying information, and unimportant details have been changed so that any resemblance to real persons is purely coincidental.

The first time a guy said to me, "Why? What should I have done differently?" when I called things off, I thought, "Really? Do I need to teach you how to be a good boyfriend?" After the third time it happened, I decided to take a break from dating and start writing.

1

Keep your eye on the prize

The most important thing to remember when dating a woman is to stay focused on your goals. If you want to have good times with her and want her to be a supportive friend to you, you have to give her what she needs to be comfortable in the relationship. Generally speaking, women will be most comfortable when:

1) we feel **special**, different from (and better than!) all you've ever dated.
2) we feel **cared for,** that you care about our feelings and our happiness. In the beginning this just means that you care about what restaurant we prefer or how we feel about saving the whales. Later it means that you care how we feel about an argument we had with a sibling, or how we feel about a situation at work. And once the relationship is serious, this will mean that you care deeply about our feelings and our happiness.
3) we feel some sense of **security** in the relationship. Not necessarily *forever* kind of security, but to know

that if we keep doing what we're doing, you'll be sticking around.

When women don't feel special, cared for, or secure, we can get jealous and annoying. When your behavior is inconsistent, we can even get crazy. This will all be discussed later on. But just remember that to get the relationship you want, you'll need to **make us feel special, cared for, and secure**. This book will teach you exactly how to do that.

Later in the book I'll be talking about a "solid relationship" and I want to take the time to define that now. A solid relationship is one where the partners know each other very well, can count on each other for friendship and support, communicate well, and are comfortable with whatever level of sexual activity they are having. It is a functioning, close relationship. It doesn't have to be serious in the sense of forever; it just has to be a close, trusting, healthy relationship for both partners.

To create a solid relationship, each partner must care about the other's happiness and act accordingly. That's really all it comes down to. Women are usually raised to be more nurturing, so it may come easier to us. That's not to say we're perfect at it, but we do have a head start. We also tend to talk with and seek advice from others on this subject. Men are great at figuring things out on their own, but that could take a bit of time. This book can help speed up the process for both men and women, leading to happier dating experiences. So guys, first thing to remember: Keep your eye on the prize, and give her what she needs.

2

Start strong

In the beginning of a relationship, it seems that men often misunderstand our need to be treated well for a need to have things get serious overnight. They somehow think that because we haven't been dating very long or aren't officially "dating" yet, they don't have to pay much attention to how they treat us.

Ryan didn't bother to call:
Ryan and Lucy met through friends and had gone out for drinks twice. They had a dinner date set for Saturday night, but were thinking of getting together earlier in the week as well. Ryan said to Lucy, "I'll give you a call later. Maybe we'll get a drink tonight." By 8PM, he hadn't called. So Lucy sent him a text, "Hey, what are you up to tonight?" At about 11PM, Ryan finally replied. He texted to say that he left the phone in his car and didn't bother to go out in the rain to get it earlier. "You're probably sleeping by now, so I'll give you a call tomorrow." Ryan didn't think it was any big deal because they hadn't made definite plans. He spent

the afternoon and evening studying for his next actuarial exam. But Lucy was expecting to hear from him. She wasn't necessarily expecting to see him, but she was expecting him to call. "If you can't follow through on calling when you say you will, it makes me doubt that you will follow through on bigger things, like our dinner date on Saturday." She didn't feel cared for, and she certainly didn't feel secure. A week later, when this type of thing happened again, Ryan said, "It sounds like you want this relationship to be serious." "Serious?" Lucy asked. "I'm not asking you to meet my parents; I'm asking for common courtesy."

What we'd like you to understand is that we (successful, intelligent, mature, sane) women are not looking to meet a guy today and be in love tomorrow. We know that good relationships take time to build and grow. But...

Nothing good will ever come from a poor start.

Even if we haven't been seeing each other for very long, you need to be sure to show common courtesy at all times. Call when you say you will call. Don't cancel plans. Don't be late. This means you have to plan ahead, account for traffic, and truly make an effort. If a delay can't be avoided, call to let us know. Little things like this make a huge difference in the beginning of a relationship. It shows that you are respectful of our time and of our feelings, which makes us feel valued and special. (You are already scoring points with us and all you've done is exhibit some common courtesy!) And keep in mind that treating us this way doesn't make the relationship serious; it makes you a good guy, and it makes us want to continue to date you.

Tom and the trip:

Tom and Amy worked together when Amy lived in New York. A few years after she moved back to the west coast, she and Tom reconnected. They both showed romantic interest and they talked about Tom visiting. The best time for him would be in January, the same time Amy had already planned a solo trip to Mexico. So, she thought about it for a couple of weeks and figured, why not invite him on the trip? It might be more comfortable to meet in neutral territory, she thought, and it will probably be more fun, too. She mentioned it to him, and he asked for more details about the trip. She was happy to forward him some information, but then, nothing. They talked several times after, and he didn't mention a thing. Finally he mentioned in passing that he'd made other plans for that week. Amy didn't feel bad about him not wanting (or being able) to come on the trip, but she was upset that he didn't ever mention it. Tom kept saying, "You're just upset because you didn't get what you wanted, me to come on the trip." But that wasn't it at all. She just wanted an answer to her question. That would have been common courtesy. "I'm sorry I can't make the trip with you, but I would love to see you soon." That's all Amy was looking for.

Kevin and his emails, part 1:

Kevin and Samantha met through an online dating website. While Kevin's interest seemed to come and go, they did end up going out once and seemed to have a great time. She didn't hear much from him afterward, and certainly no call for a second date. Oh well, she thought. About a year later Kevin saw they had a mutual "friend" online and reconnected with Samantha. She was happy to hear from him, but wondered if his interest would again come and go. The emails were short and light, with friendly conversation and a bit of flirting on his part. He mentioned getting together, and she was interested. Then, nothing. Holidays came and went, and both Kevin and Samantha were away for short vacations. After returning, Kevin wrote Samantha to ask about her trip. In fact, he wrote a second time to ask for more details. She was surprised at his level of interest, and proceeded to write back a paragraph or two. She also asked more about his trip. Then, a week went by, and nothing. Two weeks, no reply. In her mind, this was the equivalent of walking up to someone, starting a conversation, and then just turning around and walking away. *He* initiated contact after the year went by, *he* talked about making plans, *he* asked for more details about her trip, and then *he* disappeared! Clearly he still wasn't all that interested in her, but he could have at least maintained a friendship by writing a one-line email to end the conversation. Common courtesy, that's all she was looking for. Instead, she removed him as one of her online friends. And a few months later, when he tried to add her as an online friend again, she clicked "Ignore."

I know what you're thinking, "Women like bad boys." Yes, women like men who are edgy. But, of course, no woman wants to date a jerk. You can be edgy and still treat her well:

> You take us for a ride on your motorcycle. And in making those plans, you call when you say you will call, and you show up on time.

> You take us to a concert and use your connections to get us backstage. While we're backstage, you look out for us and you don't stray too far.

I'm not going to lie; the more attractive you are, the more you can get away with here. But even so, you'll never keep her if you're not treating her well. She might keep you around to sleep with you because you're hot, but when she gets tired of feeling less than special, she won't even want to sleep with you anymore. She'll call you out on your actions, you'll feel horrible, and she'll be gone.

> Jeff being late:
> Jeff and Erica met at school and they had been friends for a couple of months. Jeff kept hitting on Erica, and she finally felt comfortable enough to make plans with him. Jeff was to come to Erica's around 1PM to study and hang out. At 1, she got a text from him saying that he was going for a bite to

eat with the guys and then coming over. He arrived at her place at 4PM. While it wasn't a big deal to Erica that he came over later than planned, it didn't make her feel very special. This was their first date. And Jeff was not thinking about what would be enjoyable for her (waiting around for him?); he was only thinking about how he would enjoy having a meal with his friends before seeing her. Instead of making her feel special, he made her feel like he could take her or leave her. Not the best way to start things off. They made plans for 1PM, and he should have showed up at 1PM (and shared a meal with her!). Jeff was the most attractive guy Erica had ever dated, so she let this one slide. But, of course, it happened again. He was late for their second date, and he slept through their brunch plans (what would have been the third date). Eventually Erica just had to call things off. Yes, Jeff was hot. Yes, she enjoyed his company very much. But she deserved to be treated better than this. And his response was something along the lines of, "Relax, it's really not a big deal." Erica wasn't surprised a few months later when Jeff's new girlfriend, whom he "loved so much," dumped him too.

The bottom line here is that you need to start to think of her happiness. If you show up a half hour late to pick her up, how happy do you think she'd be? So don't do that. If she came over to watch a movie and all you have to drink is your favorite beer, she won't be as happy as if you picked up her favorite, too. In good relationships, each person looks out for the other. In the beginning, you need to start to think along these lines. If all goes well, this will be the perfect start to a solid, healthy, happy relationship. If not, at least you had some practice and you'll be even better for the next woman you date.

A Note to the Ladies: Of course, you should also start strong by treating him well, too. But treating him well does not mean you need to buy him eight Hanukkah presents when you've only been dating for a month. Don't go overboard. It's not necessary, and it will probably turn him off.

3

Put the past in the past

One of the biggest mistakes you can make in the beginning of a relationship is to remind us of women you once dated.

Do not put things in her head that you do not want to remain in her head forever.

Any information you give us about your ex-girlfriends, ex-fiancées, or ex-wives will remain in our head for all eternity. If you must talk about an ex, choose very carefully the words you use. Do not tell us about the "most amazing apartment" you found with her, the "best vacation" you took together, or how you "loved her so much." By talking about it, you are bringing the past into the present. And once it enters our head, it'll be there for our future, too. We will always compare ourselves to her. We will compare our apartment to the one you shared with her, our vacations to the vacations you shared with her, and our love to the love you shared with her. Remember that we are looking to feel special. If we are bombarded with all this from your past at the beginning of our relationship, we'll never feel special. It will be nearly impossible to overcome all the comparisons.

> Jim's perfect ring, part 1:
> Annie and Jim were excited to have found each other because of all they had in common. The first time Annie was at Jim's apartment, he mentioned that his ex used to live with him there. They had been engaged and he designed for her "the perfect ring." "No ring could be more perfect." And Annie wanted to say, "Seriously, Jim? You are excited to have met me because of the potential for a future together, and the first time I come to your place, after we sleep together, you tell me that no ring could be more perfect than the one you designed for your ex. So, the best I could ever hope for are sloppy seconds. Really, Jim?"

We don't need to know that your ex was a lawyer, that she volunteered at a nursing home, or that she did triathlons. Because the next time you mention a lawyer, a nursing home or an athlete, we're going to think of her. And thinking of her does not make us feel secure in our relationship and therefore (more importantly) it does not make things light and fun between us. (Remember, when we get insecure, we get annoying and jealous.) It also does not make us want to have regular conversations with you because when a lawyer, nursing home, or athlete comes up in conversation, we'll feel bad. Notice, the more you say about her, the more topics that will remind us of her, and the more we'll feel insecure.

We know you have a past. We just don't want to be reminded of it, at least not before our relationship is solid. Once we're feeling secure, it won't be a big deal. Think of the reverse. If we want to have good times with you, why would we ever bring up our ex-boyfriends? Why put those thoughts in your head at all?

So please do not tell us that you lived with her, or almost lived with her, or anything about her unless it directly affects us now. If she's raising your child, yes, tell us. That would directly affect our relationship. If you're paying alimony and we're talking about sharing finances, tell us. But otherwise, do we really need to know anything about her?

And if you're not fully over her and need to talk about it with a female friend, tell it to one who is not currently getting naked with you. The last thing we need to hear in the after-sex bonding moments is how you were "so in love with her." Even if we just started dating and couldn't possibly be at that point yet, we still don't want to hear it. Because we will remember that one comment six months from now when you say you are so in love with us. And we'll wonder, more than you loved her? And we'll compare. "Well, he went on vacations with her and not with me, but money is tight now so that could be a factor. He talked about living with her, but I don't know how far into the relationship that was, we're only six months in. She was a little thinner than I am, but I know he likes curves." And this will revolve in our heads indefinitely. You won't ever be able to undo it. Five or ten years down the line, we'll be having our second kid and we'll be thinking, but would he have rather married her and had kids with her? After all, he was "SO in love with her." Notice how we exaggerated the "so." The original was "so in love" and it now became "SO in love." This will always happen. Not because we are crazy or want drama, but because we want security. And whatever you say that could threaten this security will remain with us always. So please, make no mention of your former women.

A Note to the Ladies: Do not ask stupid questions, like "Did you live with anyone before?" "What did your ex do for a living?" "What was her name?" Because what will you do with this information? You'll feel bad every time you encounter someone with that name or career. You'll make up stories in your head about their relationship while they lived together. And you'll cyberstalk her.

Yes, guys, you should know about this. We can spend countless hours cyberstalking your exes. You have no idea the severity. We will find details about her even you didn't know. We'll find her Facebook, her Myspace, her current online dating profile, her employment info, and the average race pace for all her runs in the last calendar year. We'll find the pictures her mom sent to the local newspaper when she graduated college. It's out there on the internet, and we will find it. Why? Because we (foolishly) hope that by looking her up we will find something to make us feel more secure in our relationship with you. Something about how we're a better match for you. Something awful about her. Something. Anything. But what we actually find is more information to grow and take up space in our heads. More information to feed our insecurities. So please do not give us any information about these women. If they are truly in your past, it is best to leave them there.

Ladies, you must stop the cyberstalking. Nothing good ever comes of it.

And guys, maybe you think bringing up your past experiences with an ex will help make our relationship better. Maybe you want to bring up what you learned by living with her, thinking it will make it better for us as we move in together. Or maybe you think bringing up your sexual past will make our sex life better. It won't. It's great that you learned from your past, but you will have to keep those lessons to yourself. And remember, people are different. What worked for your ex may not work for us. So please, keep the past in the past. Keep us feeling good about our relationship. Keep us feeling special, cared for, and secure.

Closure

Putting the past in the past means you'll have to get rid of the perfect ring you made for your ex-fiancée, cover up that tattoo of your ex's name across your heart, and get rid of the brochures from the honeymoon you were planning together. Without getting the closure you need, you won't be able to have a successful new relationship. Even if you think you're ready, she'll feel bad knowing the ring still exists, looking at another woman's name every time you take your shirt off, or finding the honeymoon brochures when you tell her to look in your desk for a pen.

> Ari's ex addiction:
> Ari and Rachel had been seeing each other for several months, but things just didn't seem to be progressing. Rachel finally realized why. Since before they met, Ari was going online at least once a week to see that his ex-girlfriend was still on an online dating site. (It turns out sometimes the guys do the cyberstalking too.) The ex cheated on him multiple times, and it made Ari happy to see that she was single. Ari was spending all that time hating his ex and couldn't possibly be open to building something real with Rachel. Rachel got annoying and jealous, and they soon parted ways.

Moral of the story: Get your closure, and leave the past in the past.

4

The online cleanup

With the incredible popularity of social networking sites, it has become way too easy to get way too much information about the person you're dating. While it is nice to find out some things about each other (as with online dating profiles), our social networking pages often contain more information than our potential partners should see.

If you are going to add your new woman as an online "friend," keep in mind all the information she is going to find:

- The names of your ex-girlfriends
- Links to the profiles of your ex-girlfriends
- Pictures of your ex-girlfriends
- What experiences you shared with your ex-girlfriends
- How many drinks you had that awesome/horrible night
- Which of your friends was responsible for that awesome/horrible night
- How much time you spend playing Mafia Wars

- The "Wow, Beautiful!" comment you just wrote on a female friend's picture
- The "WiLD PaRtY!!" you attended on July 5th at 9:30PM
- How many hot bikini girls you met in Mexico
- How close you were sitting to the bikini girls in the hot tub in Mexico

Inviting her into your online world gives her much more information than she needs to have about you, and much more information than you may want her to have about you (especially since, you know, she probably cyberstalks). This is why I suggest the online cleanup. It's time consuming, it's boring, and it requires a lot of clicking. But you would do it before getting a new job, and you should do it before getting a new girlfriend.

At some point in your relationship (probably when you haven't called her back, when you cancel plans, or just when she's bored) she *will* read your entire online history. She'll read all the "Older Posts" until you "joined Facebook." She'll read all your blog entries and all your tweets. She'll look at all your pictures, including those in which you're tagged, the pictures you've posted yourself, and the images that come up when she googles you. It's out there and she'll find it, because she's bored, because she's curious, or because she just can't figure you out. Whatever the reason, if it's online and it's about you, she'll eventually find it.

You can choose to leave it all there, but you should know what to expect if you do:

She finds...	And then she...
The names of your ex-girlfriends	Googles them. Also googles your name with each of theirs to find any joint online info. Becomes annoying and jealous.
Links to the profiles of your ex-girlfriends	Clicks on the links. Compares herself to each ex-girlfriend. Wonders what you saw in each of them. Wonders if you still have feelings for them. Becomes annoying and jealous.
Pictures of your ex-girlfriends	Wonders if you think the exes are more attractive than she is. Assumes you have a thing for blondes with big boobs/ marathon runners/ sexy Latinas. Becomes annoying and jealous.
What experiences you shared with your ex-girlfriends	Wonders if you had more fun with them than you do with her, wonders if they were better in bed than she is, and wonders how long you dated each of them. Becomes annoying and jealous.

She finds…	And then she…
The "Wow, Beautiful!" comment you just wrote on a female friend's picture	Feels completely insecure because you haven't said that she's beautiful. Becomes annoying and jealous.
The "WiLD PaRtY!!" you attended on July 5th at 9:30PM	Wonders if that was the night you canceled plans with her. Wonders who else was at the party. Checks the names of your exes and the "beautiful" friend against the names of who attended. Becomes annoying and jealous.
How close you were sitting to the bikini girls in the hot tub in Mexico	Wonders if you slept with any of them, and wonders if you used protection. Becomes annoying and jealous.

Keep in mind that your online past is not your actual past. You are free to keep all the memories you want. I'm merely suggesting that you keep these memories off the internet. Keep the pictures on your computer or on a jump drive that your girlfriend shouldn't ever come across.

"Alexis, look at my pictures online!":
A guy Alexis dated was telling her about the fun he had on New Year's Eve with his friends back home,

20

and invited her to look at some pictures he posted online. She wasn't in the habit of looking at his page because they had only been seeing each other for about a month, and she thinks some privacy is a good thing in the beginning of a relationship. But he asked her to look at his pictures, so she did. And there was one photo of him and a female friend engaged in an innocent peck on the lips. Alexis thought it was rude and inappropriate of him to invite her to look at this photo. When she called him out on this, he went into this whole thing about jealousy. About how he can't date jealous women, blah blah blah. But it wasn't about jealousy for Alexis. She wasn't upset that he shared a peck on the lips with another woman. After all, it was New Year's Eve, and Alexis and he were only seeing each other for about a month. Alexis was upset that he posted the picture and *invited* her to see it. It was about his disregard for her and the relationship they had started. Needless to say, things didn't work out after this.

If this guy wanted to have good times with Alexis and continue seeing her, why would he put the idea of him with another woman into her head, even if she was only a friend? That would not make Alexis feel good about being with him. The idea of him with another woman would always be in the back of Alexis's mind. It would not keep Alexis's mood light and fun. And it certainly wouldn't make her feel special, cared for, or secure. He either didn't think of her feelings, or worse, tried to test her response.

The thing to remember here is to keep your eye on the prize, remember your goals. You want to have good times with us, right? Putting the idea of you and another woman into our heads is contradictory to this goal. Even if she's just a friend, even if it was New Year's Eve. If you want to keep sharing good times with us, you need to make us feel special, cared for, and secure. We want to feel good about choosing to be with you.

To be sure to keep her from getting annoying and jealous, you'd have to address the following:

Profile pictures – Delete any profile pictures of you with an ex.

Tagged pictures – Untag yourself in any pictures with an ex or with a woman you're clearly showing interest in.

Photos in your albums – Delete or change the privacy on any photos with your exes.

Your friend list – Unfriend your exes. Remember, this doesn't mean you shouldn't be real-life friends; it means you shouldn't advertise the friendship to your new woman.

Recent comments with a wink ;) – Oh the trouble those winks can cause! Compare:

> *Status post:* Thanks for all the birthday love!
> *Comment by female friend:* You're welcome :)
> vs.

Status post: Thanks for all the birthday love!
Comment by female friend: You're welcome ;)

Status post: Spring Break- a little surfing, a little adventure, and a whole lot of relaxing. Perfect.
Comment by friend: I heard there was lots of adventure!
vs.
Status post: Spring Break- a little surfing, a little adventure, and a whole lot of relaxing. Perfect.
Comment by friend: I heard there was lots of adventure ;)

If the wink can cause the comment to be interpreted in a problem-causing way, expect that to happen. Delete the comment.

Recent comments you wrote – Delete the links to any comments you've recently written. Give her less to discover.

It might seem excessive, but it's necessary if you want to keep her from getting annoying and jealous.

Julie and Ben's online drama:
Julie and Ben worked together briefly before Ben took a job about 50 miles away. They kept in touch by phone and talked about meeting up socially. Julie started to notice that Ben was calling less often, and at the same time saw that some other woman was writing all over his online page. Julie jumped to conclusions and called Ben with

questions. Ben blew up about the "drama" she started ("You're just like my mother!"). It wasn't pretty. And that was the end of Julie and Ben.

Tim's beautiful friend:
Meri and Tim were dating for about a month, and Meri was very into her social networking sites. While looking at Tim's page, she saw that "Tim commented on Karen's photo." So, of course, Meri had to click on Karen's photo to see what Tim wrote. It was a picture of Karen (whom Meri didn't know), and Tim wrote, "Wow! Beautiful!" And this made Meri feel horrible. She thought things were going well between her and Tim, but began to wonder if the attention he paid her was also being paid to other women. Meri did not feel special. Meri got annoying. And there went Meri and Tim.

I want to stress that there was nothing wrong with Tim thinking and saying that Karen looked beautiful in the picture. The problem was that he did it in such a way that Meri could see it. The relationship he had with Meri had just begun, wasn't yet solid, and this comment made her feel insecure. Nothing good will grow out of insecurity in a new relationship.

It all goes back to the logic: If you want to keep enjoying time with us, why would you put the idea of you and another woman in our head? Women (who aren't trying to play mind games with men) don't post pictures of themselves kissing other guys. We don't publicly write, "Wow! Hot!" on other guys photos. We just don't. We're interested in you, and we wouldn't want you to feel bad in any way. We want to keep having good times with you.

So, if you want to have a good relationship with us, why do something that would make us feel any less than fabulous? We understand that competition makes some men work harder and makes them more interested, but it is the opposite for women. If it looks like you're interested in or involved with another woman, we'll walk away. If we're very interested, we'll probably cry, too. (And if we think, "Game on, bitch!" then you did not pick a sane, mature, intelligent woman, and you should run far, far away.)

5

His and Hers robes

While we're on the subject of cleaning up, let's talk about cleaning house.

We know you have dated other women. We're fine with that, and we're hoping you learned something from each of your experiences. But when we're hanging out at your place, we do not want to see any signs of other women. The reason we're at your place is to hang out and have a good time. The last thing we want is to think about the other women you've brought home, or worse, the ex who used to live there with you. (This will not make us feel special, and will not make us want to get naked with you.) We know you want to be a good host, but unless you specifically went out and got that box of tampons for us, in which case it'd be unopened and our favorite brand, get rid of it.

Alan's pancakes "for company":
The first time Jenna spent the night at Alan's, he offered to make her breakfast in the morning. Whole grain pancakes. She was impressed! Alan

was cooking for her, and it was healthy! Great! But when she asked why he wasn't eating any pancakes, he replied, "Oh I don't eat pancakes. I just keep the mix for company." Company? Jenna was pretty sure Alan wasn't preparing community breakfasts on Sundays, so, what company does he make breakfast for? Oh. Right. And Jenna wondered how many others have sat in that chair in his kitchen eating the whole grain pancakes. Way to make a girl feel special, Alan.

Dan's His and Hers robes:
The first time Sandra stayed over Dan's place, she was excited to join him in his hot tub. And on their way in, Dan grabbed the robes. Yes, that's right, he had His and Hers robes for the occasion. Sandra had some more wine and enjoyed herself, but only after wondering how many other women had worn that robe (and if it had been washed since the last time!).

Steve and his shower curtain:

The first time Jessica was at Steve's place, he gave her the grand tour. The whole place felt very bachelor pad. And when they got to the bathroom, she was surprised to see cartoon character bathroom accessories. To explain, Steve said, "My ex bought those for me. We found this place together."

Problem number 1: "My ex bought those for me." OK, Steve likes cartoons. Cartoons are funny. His ex bought him a cartoon character shower curtain and a cartoon character toothbrush. Strange, but OK. Now that they have broken up and he is showing his new girlfriend around his apartment, and she's surprised to see cartoon characters in the bathroom, a better response would have been, "I love that cartoon!" He should have had the courage to say it, and the smarts not to bring up his ex!

Problem number 2: "We found this place together." Oh, where do I begin? This was Jessica's first time at Steve's place (before she was able to create any memories there with him) and she learns that he used to live there with an ex. This puts in Jessica's mind all the things Steve and his ex shared there. All the sex they had all over that apartment, all the meals they shared while sitting on that couch watching that television, and all the mornings she got to wake up in that bed with him. And knowing they found the place together puts a whole other set of memories in Jessica's head. They must have gone to realtors, looked online, or asked friends to find the place. They must have gone shopping for all the furnishings, too, since Steve also mentioned that they were both living with their parents before this.

Jessica's reaction: For the next few months, this all took up a lot of space in Jessica's head. She knew that it would take a long time for them to create as many memories there, and wondered if they would be happier memories for him. And that f***ing shower curtain. Every time she went into the bathroom she thought of his ex. *Every time.* So, one day she came over with a gift for Steve. A new shower curtain with a matching bathmat, and a new toothbrush. She went out and bought Steve new bathroom accessories. It sounds ridiculous, but it was all she could do to try to fix what Steve broke by not watching his words. I wish I could say things went well from here.

In contrast:

Jake, the dive instructor:

Lori met Jake while on vacation doing her scuba certification dives. He was one of the dive masters and was very cute, she thought! But she didn't think much of him during the first few days because there always seemed to be women around him at the dive shop. If he didn't have a girlfriend, he was probably making his way through all the tourists coming through. So Lori just went about her business and enjoyed her dives with him and the rest of the group. After she completed her last dive, he asked her out for a drink. She agreed. To her surprise, it was one of the best first dates she ever had. He said some very nice things to her and made her feel special. If he's a player, she thought, he's very good at what he does! In fact, she decided to postpone her trip home and spend more time with him. And (the reason this story is in this chapter) there were no signs of any other women at his place. Nothing purchased for the generic woman, and he didn't say one word about any ex-girlfriends ever being there. The one guy we would have expected to slip up (and not even care) was totally on his game. Be him.

So if you want to be a great host to us, get rid of anything left there by another woman, and anything you picked up with another woman in mind. Get rid of the His and Hers robes, the pancake mix for company, and anything else you bought for the generic woman. If you used to share your place with an ex, get rid of anything that prevents the place from being 100% you. Find out what we like, and pick that up for us. Your new girlfriend mentioned that she starts every day with her favorite brand of orange juice. Buy some to keep at your place. You bought it especially for her, which makes her feel special and cared for. Easy.

A Note to the Ladies: When spending time at his place, do not go fishing for information. Don't ask, "Where did you get this?" or, "Who gave you that?" He's allowed to have private memories of other women. Let him keep them private.

6

Just do it

I think we can all agree that even the best jobs require us to do things we don't always want to do. We fill out ridiculous amounts of paperwork, we attend useless meetings, and we work late nights. We don't always understand why these things are necessary, but they are easy to do and they are part of the job. We recognize what the job brings us, and accept these things as having value toward that end. Over time we might even be able to tweak the system a bit to eliminate their need.

The same is true for relationships. If you want the benefits of having someone in your life, you are undoubtedly going to have to do some things you won't always want to do. You'll have to pick her up when she could just as easily meet you there, you'll have to take your shoes off at her door, and you'll have to celebrate her birthday. You won't always understand why these things are necessary, or how they make her feel special or cared for. But they are easy to do and you will have to do them. This is a necessary part of any relationship. If you want to keep enjoying time with her, you'll have to recognize the value of these things toward that end.

Pete and Leah:
Pete and Leah started dating in mid-November. Things were going well and they were enjoying their time together, but Christmas was approaching and Leah wasn't sure what to expect. Would they see each other? And should she buy him a present? Pete was always very good about planning (and paying for) nice dates, so Leah thought it would be appropriate to pick up a gift for him. She asked to see him before they went off to their families on Christmas Eve, and he offered to stop by in the morning. He didn't stop by. He didn't call or text. He didn't call for the few days he was away, either, and one of those days was her birthday. And he didn't think this was any big deal. "You put weight into things I just don't." Leah was upset and ready to break things off, but Pete said enough of the right things to keep her on the hook. He wanted to continue dating her. He then asked about her plans for New Year's Eve. She was invited to a couple of parties, but said she'd prefer to spend the evening with him. Even though he hadn't committed to any other plans, Pete couldn't commit to spending the evening with her. He didn't understand why spending holidays together would be any big deal, and certainly wouldn't care if she forgot his birthday. He didn't realize that if he wanted to continue to see Leah, spending New Year's Eve with her was just something he'd have to do. He skipped

Christmas and ignored her birthday, and Leah needed New Year's Eve in order to feel special and cared for. But he didn't spend New Year's Eve with her, and didn't call her the next day. So on January 2nd Leah broke things off.

It's not necessary to understand every single thing about the woman you're dating. It *is* necessary to care about what's important to her, even in the beginning. This doesn't make the relationship serious; it keeps the relationship alive. As the relationship progresses, the things you have to do will be more significant. You might not have to pick her up for every date, but you'll have to attend her cousin's wedding. You'll have to bring her to your office party. And you'll have to spend the night at her place when you'd rather be together at yours.

A Note to the Ladies: It should go without saying that you will also have to do things for him. You might not understand why he needs you to watch his favorite TV show, go with him to a Super Bowl party, or go camping with his family. But these things are easy enough to do, and you will have to do them. Show up with an open mind, and you might even enjoy them. Also, pick your battles. If he agrees to attend your cousin's wedding, don't make him go dress shopping with you, too. Be considerate.

7

Dress for the job you want

We've all heard the career advice: "Dress for the job you want, not for the one you have." Well, the same holds true for your interactions with women. If there is a woman you have your eye on, but for some reason can't be with (she has a boyfriend or you work together, for example), you should be careful about the things you say and do with regard to her. You should never lose sight of the potential to be with her, and you should always be laying the groundwork to that end.

If she's not your girl right now because you work together, but you are hoping to be with her in the future, don't bring your flavor of the month to the office holiday party. Act for the relationship you want with her, not for the relationship you have with her. You think she's the greatest thing, so let her enjoy getting to know you as a potential love interest. Once you're together you won't want her to know any unnecessary information about any of your exes, so why bother bringing them around?

If she's currently seeing someone else, but you're hoping to be with her in the future, don't ask her about him and don't tell her about anyone you might be dating. I'm not saying you should be disrespectful to your current partners; I'm saying you should concentrate the conversation on other topics. It is enough for her to know that you are dating someone. She doesn't need any details. And you don't want any information about her man, information that will remain floating around in your head. So don't ask for it.

You never know when she's going to find a new job, break up with her boyfriend, or otherwise present you with the opportunity to make your move. The last thing you want is for her to have all this information about your past girlfriends and sexcapades because you weren't sure you'd ever be together. If you don't act for the relationship you want with her, even though you can't currently have it, you will likely ruin any chance of ever having that relationship.

And keep in mind that unlike men who sometimes like the competition, women do not. We won't be more interested in you knowing you have someone else. We'll be more interested in you when we see how special we are to you. It all comes back to the same things for us: We want to feel special, cared for, and secure.

8

Slow and steady wins the race

Good relationships are built on trust and a deep knowledge of one another, and this takes time. Getting too close too soon, while completely romantic and fun, can lead to a false sense of trust and understanding, and then to heartache. The hardest break-ups I've seen are of the relationships that went from 0 to 60 overnight. So while we never plan on a great relationship breaking up, we should always keep in mind the possibility, and take things slowly.

A healthy start to a relationship would have you seeing each other once or twice a week for the first few months (and not being in touch every day, not having regular 3 hour phone conversations, and certainly not texting all day long). This would allow you to slowly get to know one another *without* putting too much into the new relationship. You might think getting to know a person quickly is the best way to see if the relationship has potential. But there always needs to be a healthy balance of what is consuming your time. If all of your free time (or free thoughts!) are on this new person, the relationships you have with your friends, with your family, and with yourself are not getting enough attention. If things don't work out in your new relationship, you'll be devastated. You won't even know yourself without her, and who will help you through? The friends and family you've neglected?

> Ed gets blindsided:
> Lexi and Ed met at a concert, went home together, and so began a whirlwind romance. Vacations, family parties, and sleepovers almost every night. Then, nine months into the relationship, he has a feeling she's cheating. Ed is soon devastated to find it to be true. He loves Lexi very much. Fixated on what he thought they had, he tries to make it work. He suggests counseling; she agrees. But, yep, she does it again. Had they moved a little more slowly, he probably would have noticed either that she wasn't truly happy, or that she was the type to lie. It took Ed years to get over her (or actually, the idea of her and the romance he wanted to have with her). Years.

We often hear about people falling "madly in love" and "love at first sight." I'll expand more on this in Chapter 23, but let me just say this: You can't possibly love her if you've only known her for three weeks. You can't. You might love everything you know about her, but you can't possibly know everything you need to know in order to truly love her. And more importantly, you can't possibly care enough about her to truly love her. Love takes time.

Sometimes we like to rush into a relationship to distract ourselves from other things in our lives. Sometimes we rush into a relationship because we need to feel loved. Whatever the reason, it's probably best to deal with any underlying issues before starting a romantic relationship. The healthier we are emotionally on our own, the healthier our relationship can be.

In the beginning, the relationship should be about getting to know each other and having a good time. It shouldn't be all consuming and shouldn't feel like it is going very fast.

Maybe you can run the fast track without getting too attached too soon. But can she? Just because you can text her all afternoon and not think about her at all that night, doesn't mean she can do the same. She'll probably misinterpret your attention, thinking you care very much about her. And when she finally finds out otherwise, she'll be devastated. Confused. And maybe a little crazy!

And if she's the one speeding things up, you can always gently slow her down by being busy. Keep in mind, though, if you simply tell her "I'm busy this week," she's going to take it as a brush-off. We've been conditioned to think that *busy* means *not interested*. So if you are interested but are trying to slow things down with her, tell her about some of the things you are busy doing. Even if you are busy relaxing at home in front of the television, you can say, "With work being so hectic, sometimes I just need to spend an evening by myself." As long as you're not out with another woman, she'll be happy to wait until the weekend to see you.

A Note to the Ladies: The most important thing you can do in the beginning of a relationship is to continue to have your own life. Let the relationship develop in its own time, even if you could see a future with him and even if you're over thirty. Just enjoy your time together, and see where it goes.

9

Don't ask, don't tell (in the beginning)

We just started dating and you're curious to know if we're dating other guys. You're curious to know if we're on a dating website, or if we're getting set up by friends. So you ask, "What did you do last night?" "What are you doing this weekend?" "What are your plans tonight?" But actually it's none of your business. Don't ask us what we do every night. Don't call us every day, and don't ask us everything.

Yes, we ultimately want a committed relationship. But until we know there is potential with you, we are going to keep our options open. That's just smart. It doesn't mean we're sleeping around. It means we may take a friend up on an offer to set us up. Or we may go out knowing a friend's friend will be there. But that's not your business in the beginning, so don't ask us about it. Just be a great guy and we will choose to be with you and choose not to take up any other offers. Give it a chance, though, and try not to ask questions to which you may not want the answers. Just be present and enjoy the time you spend with us.

Similarly, don't tell us everything. We don't need to hear the play by play of your weekend, or your plans each night after work. We'll assume you are socially active and have plans with your friends. We'll assume you have a life outside of your dating life, and outside of our dates. We don't want all the details. Ignorance is bliss in the beginning. Neither of us should feel jealous of other dates or pressure to get serious. And hearing about other dates you have will certainly not make us feel special.

> Dave went ice-skating:
> Dave and Erika met at work. They immediately had chemistry, and quickly began getting to know each other. While talking on the phone and making plans, Dave mentioned that he went ice-skating the previous weekend. Now, ice-skating doesn't sound like something groups of guys would do, and probably not a mixed group either. Erika was pretty sure Dave was talking about a date he had last weekend. She still wanted to make plans with him, but was upset to think of him dating another woman. It just didn't make her feel special. If Dave wasn't talking about a date, he should have given more details. "I went ice-skating last weekend with my little sister," for example. Otherwise, telling Erika was just too much information. He shouldn't have mentioned it at all. Erika wanted to feel special, and instead felt insecure. She didn't feel comfortable on their next date, and it was their last.

If you just started seeing someone and you know she is talking to another guy, you may be turned off or jealous. You may end things before giving her a chance. Give her a little time and space. You don't want her to be with you because there are no other options; you want her to be with you because you are awesome. So just be awesome, and she will choose you. (Same advice to the ladies!)

And if you know she isn't interested in dating other guys at all, you may feel pressure to get serious too soon. So don't ask. Don't tell. Respect each other's privacy and slowly get to know each other. When you're ready, tell her that you want to be exclusive, and take it from there.

A Note to the Ladies: It may take him a few months to decide if he wants to date you exclusively. You don't want him to be your serious boyfriend just because he likes having a regular sex partner, or because he's insecure and needs a woman on his arm, do you? Or worse, just to shut you up? And I'm sure you don't want to get seriously involved with a guy who was never sure about you. You want him to want you because you're great. So, let yourself enjoy your time with him without getting all worked up about when it'll get serious. When he realizes that he consistently has a great time with you, that you are not pressuring him into a serious relationship, and that he's lucky to be dating you, he'll want to commit to you. Until then, enjoy the relationship day by day. Let him bring up exclusivity when he's ready. If he hasn't brought it up after a few months, you might want to start the conversation. But by then you should also be aware that you two might not want the same things, and the relationship might soon end. So until he brings it up, enjoy your time with him but keep your options open. Go out and meet people. Live your life, and don't put too much weight on the developing relationship you have with him. If it turns into something lasting, that's great. But if not, you want to have enough of a life without him to get you through the break-up.

10

Confidence

This chapter is about having the confidence to truly be yourself. To speak your truth, to act your truth, and to be your true self every day. It's also about recognizing your true value.

Firstly, I must address the constant apologizer. If you're the guy who is always apologizing to women for things you've done, please listen up. Either accept the man you are and stop apologizing for it, or be a better man and stop doing those things for which you feel the need to apologize. Either we'll love you for who you are, or we won't. But we won't be able to figure that out until you decide on who you want to be. Be yourself, or be better. Those are your options. Pick one, and stop apologizing. Until you do, we'll be your crying, annoying girlfriend.

Secondly, I want to address the guys who are afraid to let their true selves be known. The guys who are busy trying to be what they think women want them to be, and who hardly ever get to be themselves. If you don't think this woman would be interested in you as you are, why on earth would you want to be with her? If you change into someone who wears fancy clothes, listens to her favorite music and suddenly loves tennis, all to please her, how long do you think you two will be happy together? This can't possibly be sustainable. Either you'll be unhappy (and perhaps resentful), or your true colors will start to show and she won't be happy. It's one thing if she makes you want to be a better man, if she's a reason to be your best self, but it's something entirely different if she wants someone you're just not. So please, be yourself. And make no apologies for it! We're pretty sure that when you don't judge yourself for the little things, you're not going to judge us, either.

Lastly I want to address those guys who seem confident on the outside, but who are driven by their insecurities. These are the guys who pride themselves on their looks, their great gym-bodies, and their smooth ways with the ladies. And the guys defined by their money or power. If these are the attributes that you feel give you the most value and the most confidence, you will never be in a happy, successful relationship. Your value comes from your character. I'm going to say it again:

Your value comes from your character.

If you rely on your looks, your money, or your achievements to bring you self-esteem, it will never be enough. Your value comes from how you treat other people. It comes from the relationships you make, and the people whose lives you touch. When you focus on other things to bring you value and confidence, you will always be looking for more. No amount of money, power, or women can fill that void. It just can't.

And unless your values are straightened out, you'll never be able to have a happy, successful relationship. You'll always feel insecure, and will always be searching for more attention from women, more money, or more power. And when you meet a woman who loves you for who you are (regardless of your extra weight, your thinning hair, or your recent pay cut), you'll be focusing on the wrong things and you'll lose her. Instead of focusing on being good to her, you'll feel bad about whatever you lack. You won't truly be self-confident, you won't treat her well, and you will lose her.

Unless you can find true value in the person you are *without* the things you have, your achievements, or your looks, I don't believe you'll ever truly be happy, and I certainly don't believe you can sustain a happy, successful relationship. Because when we know you accept yourself and find great value in yourself, we know you have the ability to accept us and find great value in us.

> Mark's insecurities:
> When Mark met Alicia, he didn't realize she was six years older than him. He was finishing up grad school, and she had already made some headway in her career. They got along very well, and Alicia was excited to have met him. She always had a great time with him and enjoyed getting to know him. But as they got closer, Mark would say things like, "You're so much more successful than I am. I have

nothing to offer you." And it soon became clear that this was an issue for Mark. He wasn't comfortable dating her. Alicia was heartbroken. She liked him more than any guy she'd ever met. She didn't care that he didn't have much money or start his career yet. She knew things would eventually work out for him and wasn't concerned about it in the least. She always had a great time with Mark and always felt she could be 100% herself around him. This was much more valuable to her than his career status. If only he had some confidence.

A Note to the Ladies: It's always nice to say things to make a person feel good about him/herself. Especially if you think his confidence could use a boost, tell him what he's good at. Tell him what you value about him. Why not let him know what's on your mind if it would make him feel good to hear it?

11

Reading the signs

Some women like to always be in relationships because they don't like being alone. So how can you tell if she's truly interested in you?

If her behavior is a little questionable, she's either not that interested in you, or just too self-involved to really care about you.

- She only calls or texts when she wants something, not to say hi or to see how your day is going.
- She won't commit to plans with you until the last minute, after she sees what her friends are up to (unless you're taking her to an expensive restaurant, to see a show, on vacation, etc.).
- When she talks about the future, rather than ask what you want, she assumes you'll want everything she wants.
- She somehow gets you to buy her fancy clothes and material things that, really, she should buy for herself. ("Oh, I'd love to go to that fancy party with you, but I don't have anything I could wear.")

If she's not that interested in you but just wants your attention, she may get annoying. But be sure you understand the reason and let her go. This is not your fault, and you can't fix it. You can't make a woman want you any more than we can make you want us.

A Note to the Ladies: If you're truly not that interested in him, don't lead him on. Respect his feelings and offer him the same courtesy you'd expect from him.

When she is genuinely interested, you won't have to question it. You'll know.

- Even though she may not "chase" you and initiate contact, she's always happy to hear from you.
- She wants to spend time with you. Not so you can spend money on her, just because she likes being with you. It makes her feel good to be around you. She's comfortable with you.
- She respects you and the choices you make. She'll seek to understand your choices rather than ever judge you or put you down for them.
- She accepts you for exactly who you are. She'll never make you feel like you're not attractive enough, that you don't make enough money, that you aren't smart enough, or that you don't come from a good enough family.

Another Note to the Ladies: These are the same signs you should look out for with guys, with one exception. If he's not doing the chasing, he's not that interested.

12

Texting

We love technology as much as you do. Really. But we see texting as a supplemental form of communication. You need to call us. Call when you want to make plans. Call if you are running late. Call to see how our day was. Text on your way home from our date to say, "I had a great time." Text if you know we're busy at work. Text if you know we're sleeping.

Because texting is an easy way to pay someone attention, it doesn't make us feel special at all.

> Day 3 Dylan:
> Joy had a great first date with Dylan. He texted her on his way home to say he had a great time. She wrote back saying she did as well. She was happy to have had a good time on a first date! The next day, she didn't hear from him. Another day passed, still nothing. On the third day she got a text saying, "So, how do we feel about getting together again?" A *text*? *Three* days later? Gee, Dylan, way to make a girl feel special. If Dylan had *called*, even on the

third day, Joy would have been happy to go out with him again. But in this case, she lost interest and passed on the second date. Strange thing was, Dylan tried repeatedly over the course of the next six weeks to get her to go out with him again. So it seems he actually was interested! But it was *all by text*. And Joy's lost interest never returned.

Also worth mentioning here, a little text etiquette: If you need to end one of our text-chats, don't just stop texting. You wouldn't just get up and walk away without saying goodbye, would you? If our last text warrants a comment or asked a question, and you just stop texting, we take that as a dismissal. We understand you're busy, no problem. Just type "gotta go, ttyl." Otherwise we're going to keep checking the phone, feel completely dismissed, and think you're a jerk.

A Note to the Ladies: If you're in the habit of texting often with your friends, you might think nothing of texting your new guy at random times just to say hello or just to see what he's doing. Resist the urge. Do not chase him by text. Unless he is needy for attention, it will seem to him that you are, and he'll begin to lose interest.

13

Online dating

Oh, the joys of online dating. What could theoretically be the most efficient way of meeting like-minded people is definitely the most impersonal. And because of that, it's very important to get things right in the online dating world.

The single biggest turn-off we find online is when a guy writes in his profile that he's looking to meet "girls" or "women." Sure, you'll probably have to meet more than one of us to find one you like, but remember that we want to feel special. Writing that you are looking for women (plural) makes us think you are looking for a harem. We're probably not into that. So if you are, in fact, ultimately looking for one woman with whom to share your time, don't make us think otherwise.

The second biggest turn-off we find is a poor choice of pictures. The first ones you can get rid of are the ones of you in front of a sunset or at a fancy party with your ex-girlfriend cut out. We don't want to see her long flowing blonde hair on your shoulder. We don't need to see the super-romantic candlelit sunset dinner you shared in

Greece. These things will just make us feel insecure later on. If those are truly the only good pictures you have, then before you sign up for online dating you need to do what women do. Make a night out with your friends specifically to take pictures. Yes, we do this. When we get tired of the pictures we have online, we say to one another, "I need some new pictures to post. Let's go out tonight." We go out, we have a great time, and we take lots of pictures. So if you need some good pictures, make a guys night out. Look your best, and take lots of pictures. Get women at the bar to take your picture (two birds one stone, thank you). Some of the pictures will be good. Some of them will be funny. Perfect.

The next turn-off we find is when all of your pictures have you wearing a hat or sunglasses. Firstly, we can't see what you truly look like. We want to see the real you. Secondly, if you're losing your hair, own it. Show us how great you look anyway.

Now, with this next issue I almost want to tell you to have your pictures approved by one of your female friends. Because posting a picture of yourself wearing an "FBI: Female Body Inspector" t-shirt is never a good idea. Let's use this as a rule of thumb: If you wouldn't wear it on a date, don't post a picture of yourself wearing it on a dating website. (And if you would wear that FBI t-shirt on a date, you deserve a kick in the head. Really.)

Another big online dating turn-off is when you send a "wink" or a "flirt" rather than writing us an email. Man up. Gather some words of your own and write us something personal. Go for it. We want to see your confidence and personality shine through.

And when you're writing us, the last thing we want to see is the copy-and-paste letter:

> Hi there, I enjoyed reading your profile. You seem interesting and it seems we have some things in common. I would love to know more about you. As for me, I have been living here for 2 years now. I moved here from Florida where I grew up. I am a pretty simple guy and would love to find my best friend. Not sure what else to write but feel free to ask me anything.
>
> Hope to hear from you soon. Are you on Facebook?

The first thing we notice about this letter is that he didn't write one thing about her profile that he liked. The letter is completely generic. When you are initiating contact with a woman online, you want to connect with her. Find one of the "interesting" things in her profile and connect with her about it. For example,

> Hey there,
> I enjoyed reading your profile. I also love to travel. Where were those photos taken? Any trips coming up? I just came back from Costa Rica. Would love to tell you about it sometime.
> Josh

Another important tip is to always ask at least one question. It shows your interest and is an easy way of keeping the conversation going. If you do all the talking about yourself, you don't seem interested in us, and we'll have nothing to say. So ask us a question! But, just as you'd be careful on a date not to sound like you're interviewing someone, give the same care to the questions in your emails. The email from Josh above, asking about her travels, is a great example. He's not asking, "Are your parents still together? Do you believe in God? What do you think of the latest political scandal?" He's simply asking about something she has already posted in her profile. He's acting interested while staying within her comfort zone.

Speaking of comfort zone, notice the first email above asks about Facebook. For many of us on dating websites, anonymity is important. Particularly for women, it is also a safety issue. Until we get to know you, we're not going to want to give you our full names or our regular email addresses. It would be better to stick to the anonymous email from the dating site until we get to know you better.

The most important piece of advice I can give, though, is to be yourself. Don't send an email someone else wrote for you. Don't let someone else write your profile. You want to find someone who likes you for you. So put your true self out there, be confident, and see what comes your way.

14

Long distance relationships

With long distance relationships, all possible forms of communication are significant. Phone and email are the basics, but it's great if you can video chat and text message as well. And since you're not spending time together on a regular basis, it's important to find time to communicate often. This can be difficult, especially if there's a difference in time zone or work schedule, but it is essential.

> Greg's theater work:
> Greg was in theater production and typically took jobs that would take him out of town for a month or two at a time. He would usually spend at least as much time home in between jobs. When he met Shannon, he had just returned home from a job. They spent a great 6 weeks together before he headed out again. Shannon accepted his career and was willing to make it work while he was away. But things were very different while Greg was gone. He was working 80+ hours per week, including late nights. Besides the difficulty of finding common time to talk on the phone, Greg's needs in the

relationship had changed. He no longer was interested in hearing about Shannon's days, and no longer wanting to share about his. He was focused on work and "too busy" to be in touch regularly. When Shannon said she was willing to accept his being away for work, she didn't know it meant accepting that Greg's needs were going to be very different. Since Shannon's needs hadn't changed, they needed to compromise. Greg wasn't willing, and the relationship ended.

The most important thing here is to recognize what you both need and expect from the relationship. It might be that you are happy with one solid phone conversation per week, and perhaps some texts or short emails in between. If the relationship has progressed some, you might want to be in touch more regularly. Whatever the situation, be sure to be open about your expectations, either at the start of the relationship or as soon as you see your expectations are not being met.

This is particularly important with email communication.

Dana's "book":
John and Dana met their freshman year in college, and started dating soon after. As part of his degree, John needed to do a summer semester at sea. John could call Dana while in port, but while at sea they were limited to text-only emails. A few weeks into his trip, he opened her latest email and his jaw dropped. "She wrote me a f***ing book." Tired, he read half of it, didn't reply, and logged out. When

Dana didn't get a reply, she got insecure. And she wrote more long emails, now about her feelings. John and Dana clearly had different expectations about their email communication while he was at sea.

If email is our primary form of communication, you have to read our emails and *answer all of the questions*. You have to. Don't assume you'll remember to answer those questions when we talk on the phone, because you won't. If you don't answer all of our questions, we're going to feel ignored. And then we'll get annoying.

We understand you are away for a reason, that you're busy. Or that you have a life outside of the long distance relationship. But if we are not important enough for you to spend time writing us a nice email or talking to us on the phone, we can only imagine how you'll treat us when life gets busy at home. "Too busy" means you're not that interested. And that is true whether you are home or away. Don't take for granted that we will be there when you get back, or that we'll want to continue the long distance thing. We might hang around for a little while, but being repeatedly ignored wears us down and eventually we'll be gone.

A Note to the Ladies: Although I did suggest that he answer all of the questions in your email, I'm also going to suggest that you try your best not to write him a book. Be sensitive to his position, and try to say it all in fewer words.

15

The more you give, the more you have

Good relationships of any kind (romantic relationships, friendships, familial relationships) are based on giving. It's not about money and buying physical things; it's about giving your time and energy. Think about the people in your life with whom you want to have a good relationship. Think about something nice you can do for each of those people. Probably these things wouldn't cost you much in time, effort, or energy. And doing these things will not only make them smile, but will make you feel like the greatest brother, son, friend, boyfriend (or sister, daughter, girlfriend) etc.

One of the biggest problems women find with men is selfishness. And we're constantly looking for men who will base their actions on things other than what they need and want in the moment. We're not suggesting a guy should live totally for us and lose himself. We want a partner who has a life and interests and an opinion of his own. But when we find a guy who is his own person *and* who genuinely cares about our happiness, we know we found a keeper.

Zack wasn't hungry:

Zack and Jenn had been dating for a couple of months. Jenn was heading to Zack's after a busy day. She had a long workout in the morning and had been running errands all day. She was starving. She called Zack to let him know she was on her way over, and asked him to order food. He agreed. When she got to his apartment, there wasn't any food; he didn't order anything. He told her that he wasn't hungry and figured they could wait until later to eat. He then started kissing her, thinking he'd get some action. He knew Jenn was starving and said he'd order food, but changed his mind solely based on what would make him happiest at that moment. Jenn clearly did not feel cared for. She put a quick stop to his advances and they went out to get some dinner. She was annoyed (and annoying) for days, until she felt cared for again.

While Zack might be able to find a woman to put up with this, she certainly won't be the kind of woman I am talking about here. She'll be lonely and desperate and happy to have found a warm body to pay her attention. Because no self-respecting woman would put up with a guy who would disregard her wants and needs.

In contrast:

Jared was listening:

Lisa mentioned to her friend Jared that since she was new in town, she had no one to spend the holidays with. The next week, Jared invited her to spend the holidays at a friend's house with him.

Lisa was surprised Jared even remembered what she said, since she just mentioned it in passing. Another time, Lisa mentioned that, again, being new in town, she didn't have any friends who enjoyed outdoor activities. He called her a couple of weeks later and invited her to go kayaking. The thing to note here is that these were things Lisa mentioned only in passing. Jared was paying attention to what she said, and later acted on it. When she mentioned to him that she recognized and valued this about him, he said something about how it makes for a more full relationship. Jared made Lisa feel cared for. And Jared quickly moved out of the friend zone.

Being generous with your time and energy can make *all* the difference between a woman falling for you or not. Doing thoughtful things for her will put you on the fast track to her feeling special, cared for, and secure. Taking the time and energy to do something nice and unnecessary will make her feel special (since it is just for her) and cared for (since you care about how it makes her feel). If you do things like this regularly, she will see consistency in your behavior and begin to feel secure.

Once you get to know her, you'll be able to do these nice little things for her. This doesn't mean you have to spend lots of money, it means you have to think of things that would make her smile. Non-sexual things.

Here are some ideas:

- If you two will be hanging out at your place, pick up her favorite beverage.
- Help her find a parking spot or clear your driveway for her.
- If she mentioned in passing that she's always wanted to hike a certain trail or go wine tasting, plan it as a date! We *love* to realize that you were actually listening when we spoke. Seriously. Big points for that.
- Call and ask how her day is going.
- If she is stressed about something and seems a little overwhelmed, ask if you can help.

Think about what would make her smile, and make an effort to do these things. It'll probably take a month or two for you to get to know what she likes. But once you do, show that you are thinking of her when she's not around. We *love* that. And I'm not trying to say you should buy her things. This isn't about money. Give what you can give. If it's time you have, then take the time to find a new restaurant you think she'd love, an independent movie she'd want to see, or even just help her find a store that sells her favorite swim goggles. If you're short on time but have lots of nightlife connections, for example, make a few calls and set something special up. Work with what you have. You can always do something extra that would bring a smile to her face.

Dean and Donna moving:

Dean and Donna had been dating for about a year when they decided to move in together. Donna was almost done packing her stuff when she received devastating news. A death in the family. She left the next day to be with her family for the week, but she still needed to move out. Of course, Dean finished her packing and moved her things to the new place. But after the move, Dean took it a step further. He offered to unpack all of her things for her via video-chat so she could tell him where everything goes. He didn't want her to have to come home from a difficult week only to begin unpacking. Just another reason Donna loves Dean.

Even if you can't think of something specific to do for her, if she seems stressed with work or not feeling well, for example, ask her: "What can I do to help you?" More often than not, it will be something simple like picking up her dry cleaning and a box of cereal. Easy, and you're a great boyfriend.

A Note to the Ladies: When he does something nice for you, appreciate it. Thank him. Let him know that you recognize the effort he made. And when you are doing nice things for him, again I need to remind you not to go overboard. Bringing him groceries when he's sick is a nice gesture. Bringing him groceries every weekend is not appropriate.

16

Creating memories

One of the best things you can do to help us feel special is to create new memories with us. Take us somewhere you've never been before, or do something with us you've never done before. Knowing that you've chosen to include us in this new experience makes us feel very special to you.

This is especially important if you've had significant relationship experience before us. If you have lots of memories with your exes (vacations, living together, even a wedding), you'll need to create special memories with us, too. We want to know that when you think back to the good times in your life, we were there. We want to be significant to you. We want to be special.

With this in mind, it's important not to make us feel like just a replacement for your ex. So if we're always eating dinner at the same restaurant you went to with your ex every week, or we've just taken her place as your regular Friday night date, we're not going to feel special at all.

Scott's repeat vacation:

Scott had been scuba diving since he was 16, and Emma recently took the certification class. They were planning their first trip together, one where she could do her certification dives. She asked him to suggest a destination. Of all the places in the world to dive, he suggested Bonaire, where he had traveled with his ex. He even suggested the same resort. Emma asked if he wanted to arrange for the same hotel room, as well, so they could sleep in the same bed. She then tried explaining to Scott that she wanted to create new memories with him, not relive his old ones. He didn't see how it was any big deal. They split soon after, never taking a vacation together.

We understand that some people like to do what's comfortable and shy away from the unknown. We also understand that you might have a favorite restaurant or a favorite vacation spot. We're not opposed to experiencing these things with you; we just want to have some of our own memories with you first. So when we are planning our first vacation together, don't suggest a resort or even a destination you've been to with an ex, even if it is your favorite. Save that trip for next year. Because when we get to the same destination and all your memories are revived (and they will be!), we'll feel insecure. We'll compare our trip to your trip with her, and we'll compare our relationship to your relationship with her. It would be better to wait until our new relationship is solid before putting us in that position. By then we'll be secure in the relationship, and it won't be a big deal. But until then, create new memories with us by choosing something new.

A Note to the Ladies: Keep in mind that not all new memories you create together will be romantic vacations. He may need a hand repainting his apartment or choosing a birthday present for his mom. Be open to creating a variety of new memories, and cherish them all.

17

The Chosen One

At any stage in the relationship, it's important to let a woman know why you're dating her. Let her know why you choose her. We want to feel as though you're dating us for a reason, not just because we happen to be there. We want to know that we are special to you in some way, and that if we keep doing what we're doing, you'll keep choosing us. Because if you can be interested in anyone who's reasonably cute, for example, we know we can be easily replaced and won't feel secure. (And when we don't feel special or secure, we get annoying and jealous.)

So, we need to hear the words. In the beginning it can be as simple as:

> "I feel good when I'm around you."
> "You're very easy to talk to."
> "I love how much we laugh when we're together."

Then once you get to know us better, maybe:

> "You're very supportive and you make me feel good about myself."
> "I know I can always count on you."

"I'm inspired by how much you've accomplished."
"I'm happy when I'm with you."

And, whenever appropriate, add on to any of the above:
"... and I've never had that before."

Ah, the "I've never had that before." This one line makes us instantly feel valued and special. Use it well. (Of course, you should only say it if it is true.)

Without hearing why you choose to be with us, we'll feel like you'd date anyone. We'll think you don't have any standards or anything in particular you're looking for, and that you're just looking for a warm body in your bed.

> Doug and the vacation house:
> Doug and Rosa met at the vacation house they shared with a large group one summer. By the end of the first week, they had spent quite a bit of time together and Doug went in for the kiss. They enjoyed another few weeks of each other's company until Rosa found out that a couple of days before he made a pass at her, he made a pass at another woman in the house (who wasn't interested in him). At first Rosa felt like his second choice, but got over it after realizing that he met the other woman first. What Rosa couldn't get over, however, was how different this other woman was from her. Doug and Rosa were both in their early thirties, both accomplished and successful in their careers. Both well traveled with lots of life experience. This other woman was 10 years

younger, a normal young twenty-something, just starting out. Rosa just couldn't figure out how he could be attracted to both of them, as they were quite different. "He can't possibly value all that I have to offer if he could have just as easily dated her. He can't possibly be interested in something real with me." It was a summer house, after all. But Rosa was thinking much more about this than Doug ever had. Doug was in fact interested in something real with Rosa, and soon realized that he needed to tell her what he found special about her. (A smart man, he also gave Rosa reasons he was happier with her than he would have been with the young twenty-something.)

We need to hear what it is you like about us, and what makes us different from other women to you. If you can't articulate anything that makes us special to you, then it feels like we're just the flavor of the month. We want to know that we're the one you choose, and that if we keep doing what we're doing, you'll keep choosing us.

18

"I'm sorry"

Somewhere along the way, someone told you how important it is to say "I'm sorry" to a woman when you've done something wrong. I disagree. Because if you just slept through our brunch plans, what is an "I'm sorry" going to do? It's going to make *you* feel better, not us. Instead of saying you're sorry, you need to *fix it*. Whatever you did for which you are now sorry, you need to not do that again, and you need to make up for it by making *us* feel better.

So when you do something worthy of an apology, think about the underlying issue. Why is she upset? Did you make her feel not special? Did you make her feel not cared for? Did you make her feel insecure?

And take action to repair what you broke. Besides not doing it again, there's usually something extra you can do to show that you are changing your ways. Make the effort to do this. It will save your relationship.

Some examples to follow, but first:

A Note to the Ladies: If he's doing any of the following in the very beginning of your relationship, he's probably not that interested in you and just wants to sleep with you. (Sorry.) But if he does one of these after you've been dating for a few months or longer, it is probably a legitimate mistake. And in that case, once he makes proper amends, *let it go!*

Some examples and how to make amends:

> *Why you're sorry*: You slept through brunch plans.
> *Why she's upset*: She feels as though you don't care if you see her. She doesn't feel cared for or special.
> *How to make amends*: Make sure it doesn't happen again. Set your alarm clock, set your phone's alarm, and keep your phone's ringer on so you'll hear her call in the morning. Make plans with her a priority. Cancel some other plans to make up for the date you missed.

> *Why you're sorry*: You showed up late to a date.
> *Why she's upset*: She feels as though you don't value her time, and therefore don't value her. She doesn't feel cared for or special.
> *How to make amends*: Don't show up late again. Call on your way to let her know where you are, so she won't worry that you'll be late again.

> *Why you're sorry*: You paid inappropriate attention to another woman.

Why she's upset: She's looking for security and you've just threatened that. She's not sure you still want to be with her. She doesn't feel special. She feels disrespected by you (and not cared for).

How to make amends: Don't do this again. And pay your woman extra attention so she knows you want her. Be sure to show concern for her feelings in general. Do some nice things for her so she feels cared for and special.

Why you're sorry: You didn't call when you said you would.

Why she's upset: She's not sure you're still interested in her. She wonders if you can keep other, more important, commitments. She doesn't feel special or cared for.

How to make amends: If you can't always call when you'd like (because of unexpected things at work, for example), let her know. And next time, give her your back-up plan. "I'll call you Tuesday night or Wednesday afternoon." Do some nice things to let her know you are thinking of her.

Why you're sorry: You cancelled a date so you could go out with your friends.

Why she's upset: She's not sure you're still interested in her. She doesn't feel special or cared for.

How to make amends: Only cancel a date to hang out with your friends when the plans with your friends are significant, like someone's big birthday/bachelor party, when there's a big game to watch, or when someone is in town only for the weekend. And explain to her why going is important to you. She shouldn't be upset in this case.

Why you're sorry: You ran into your ex while together, and didn't introduce her.

Why she's upset: She doesn't feel significant at all. She doesn't feel special.

How to make amends: Introduce her to some friends she hasn't met, or bring her to a work party. Make it clear that she is special enough to be introduced to people in your world. If you run into your ex again, be sure to introduce her.

The bottom line here is this. You are in this relationship by choice. Whether you just started dating her or have been together a long time, you are choosing to be in the relationship. And with that, you have to treat her right. You have to give her what she needs in the relationship. If you mess up (because, hey, nobody's perfect), then you have to make it right. You have to make your amends.

Another Note to the Ladies: Of course, we'll need to make amends at times, too. It never hurts to say the words "I'm sorry," but be sure to do whatever you can to make him feel better, and be sure not to make the same mistake again.

80

19

"Everybody makes mistakes"

This is true. Nobody is perfect, and everybody makes mistakes. But let's get something clear right now. Sleeping through brunch plans is a mistake. Sleeping with another woman is a conscious choice.

Mistakes are what we make when we're not thinking clearly about what we're involved in. You had a tough day, you went out for a drink with your buddies, and you forgot to set your alarm for the next morning. It happens.

Or maybe you ran into an ex unexpectedly and fell into the old habit of flirting with her in the moment. But you quickly realized that it was inappropriate and changed your ways. That would count as a mistake. Once the surprise of running into her wore off, you were thinking clearly and chose not to flirt with her.

Making mistakes is expected and understandable in relationships. Making conscious choices that disregard your partner's feelings is not.

Let's compare:

Mistakes (acceptable)	Conscious choices (unacceptable)
Danced a little too hot and heavy with that one girl at that one club for that one song on that one night	Consistently going out and dancing up on other women, knowing you wouldn't appreciate if we did the same with other guys
Sent a few flirty texts to one other woman that one night when you were feeling down on yourself	Consistently sending flirty texts to the same other woman, or regularly sending them to a variety of women
Met someone at the bar and took her number (and then later deleted it, knowing you'd never call)	Met someone at the bar and took her number, texted her that night, and made plans to get together Or worse, Met someone at the bar and went home with her
Making plans with a female friend and calling it a "date"	Making plans with a female friend and acting like it's a date by touching her, trying to kiss her, etc.

Defending cheating (or the other conscious choices listed) with "everybody makes mistakes" is like saying, "Oh, I wasn't paying attention. I thought I was naked in *your* bed." Or, "I thought I was sending sexy texts to *your* phone for the past two months."

In reality it was probably more like "She's hot. I know she's not my girlfriend but I don't really care." And that is a choice. At that moment and in the moments to follow, you chose to disregard the feelings of your partner. This is contradictory to the whole concept of being in a relationship. If you can't or don't want to be aware of your partner's feelings and act accordingly, *you shouldn't be in the relationship*.

But if the thought of losing your partner over this makes you think twice and realize you should have chosen differently, you'll probably need to do some work to rebuild what you broke. The next chapter (Trust) will help you do just that.

Now if you've made a mistake and you're sure it won't happen again, it's probably best not to tell her. You don't want to put things in her head that she doesn't need to have in her head. If your relationship is healthy and trusting, she should understand if she ever found out. *However*, if you have previously broken her trust (see next chapter) then you should tell her.

I can't end this chapter without mentioning, however, that if the list of conscious choices looks a little too familiar to you, there are probably some issues that need to be worked out.   Relationships are about giving, and if you're more concerned with the attention or care that you are getting, you're probably not ready to be in a relationship.

20
Trust

Remember that we are looking for security. We want to know that if we keep doing what we're doing, you'll be sticking around.

Security and trust are hugely related. If any of the things you tell us are not true, we have no reason to believe you when you talk about being happy in our relationship, being exclusive, etc. If you are someone who sometimes lies, you know where your line is. You know when you feel it's OK to tell a lie, and when you feel you must be truthful. But we'll never know where that line is for you, and we'll never know what to expect from you. Not knowing what to expect from you is the opposite of security. And remember, when we don't get what we need from you, we get annoying, jealous and perhaps even crazy. Or, we just leave.

So if you want to have a happy, successful relationship with us, we need to know we can trust you. And to see if we can, we'll be looking for different things as the relationship progresses.

If we just started dating:

> We need to see that you **keep your word**. Call when you say you are going to call. Show up where you say you are going to show up. If you've invited us somewhere, take us there. If you've offered to lend us something, follow through and lend it to us. Consistency between your words and your actions makes us feel secure.

> We need to see that your **actions are consistent**. If you've been calling twice a week in the evening for the two months we've been dating, and then you stop, we're going to wonder why. We'll no longer feel as though we know what to expect from you, and no longer feel that security. (If, for example, you're working late one week and can't call, simply let us know. Addressing the issue lets us know that you recognize the value of being consistent.)

If we just started being exclusive, or you would like to be exclusive:

> Now is when the foundation of trust is built for the relationship. This is when we start to become closer emotionally.

> We need to see that you **tell the truth**. As mentioned above, if you are the type of person who lies, we'll never know what to expect from you. We'll never know where the line is for you between speaking the truth and lying. We won't be able to

believe the things you say about anything. We'll wonder if we are exclusive or not, if you really were too tired to go out, if you really had plans with your buddies last night, or if you really were just on the phone with your mom. It is *very important* at this point in the relationship to tell the truth about everything.

We need to see that you are **open about your life**, and aren't hiding anything. We don't need to know how much money you make or why your parents got divorced, but we'd like to know that you're open to sharing with us what's going on in your life. Instead of saying, "I have plans with a friend tonight," say what the plans are, and with whom. "I'm having dinner with my friend Joe/Jen from work. There's a new Thai place we want to try." Just hearing that you have "plans" makes us think you don't want us to know what you're up to. And if it makes you uncomfortable to be that open with us, perhaps you're not ready to take the relationship to the next level.

We need to see that your **actions and words are consistent**. Now it's more than just calling when you say you'll call. If you tell us, "I'd love for my parents to meet you," but then you don't invite us the next three times you have dinner with them, that's inconsistent. We'll wonder if you were telling the truth about wanting them to meet us. We'll wonder if you changed your mind about it. And the wondering is the problem. If we don't know what to expect, we're not feeling secure. And now that we're just starting to build something, it is more important than ever for us to feel like we're starting to know you and to know what we can expect from you. (If there is a reason you don't invite her one particular time, just be sure to address the issue. Let her know why. This shows that you would still like for your parents to meet her, which shows consistency.)

We still need to see that **your actions are consistent**. Earlier in the relationship, seeing that your actions were consistent was about you calling consistently and seeing us consistently. But now that emotions are beginning to get involved, it is even more important that we see consistency in your actions. For example, if you've made a habit of sleeping at our place after our Saturday night dates, and then suddenly you want to sleep alone in your own bed, that's inconsistent. We're going to wonder why, and we'll probably feel insecure unless you mention why.

We need to see that **you start to look out for us**. This is a big one. As we're starting to build a relationship, we're looking to see now that we can trust that you care about us. We want to see that you have our best interests at heart. It's more than just doing nice things for us; it's about looking out for things that are important to us:

- If we're sick, offer to run a couple of errands for us.

- If we are having a problem at work, ask us about it.
- If you invite us to a concert of a band we don't know, download some songs for us so we can better enjoy the show.
- If you know we've had a tough week, consider rescheduling our double date with your friends and just plan a DVD night for this weekend.
- If you know we love our Saturday morning yoga class, try planning our late date nights on Saturdays rather than Fridays.

Rebuilding trust after it has been broken:

If you have made any of the "conscious choices" in the last chapter, or anything else that could have broken our trust in you, you'll undoubtedly need to do some work to rebuild what you broke. But even if all you ever did was lie about where you went last night, we'll still wonder if you've ever cheated. Again, we don't know where the line is for you with lying or with breaking your word. We don't know what we can believe or when we can trust you.

And just as the one thing you tell us about your ex will remain in our heads for all eternity, so will the one (or two or three) thing(s) you did to break our trust. We will constantly wonder whom you are texting, if you really were working late, really out with the boys, or really stuck in traffic. The best thing you can do to earn back the trust is to be very open about everything you are doing.

If you broke her trust in a serious way, like cheating, she does not have to trust you again simply because you say you're "sorry." She'd be a fool to do so. If you truly are worthy of her trust, you'll need to understand that it will only be built back up by showing that things are different, i.e. by proving that you aren't having private contacts with another woman. This means you'll need to be comfortable checking email in front of her, letting her use your phone, and leaving her in your apartment while you run out for coffee. She needs to consistently see that you have nothing to hide.

Remember that we are looking for security. The sooner we can trust you, the sooner we'll feel secure and the happier our relationship will be.

A Note to the Ladies: If he does leave you at his place while he runs out for coffee, you should *not* take it as an invitation to snoop. Snooping will always lead to misunderstandings, and can easily ruin a relationship. Also, unless you have reason to believe otherwise, you have to take him at his word. You have to believe what he says. He is not your lying ex. Give him the chance to show you what kind of guy he is.

21

Fight for her

We know that when we tell you to go away, to stop calling, and to leave us alone that you think we really mean it. That's only partly true. What you need to understand is that if we say those things *after* being hurt by you in some way, what we actually want is for you to stop doing that which hurt us, and stick around. We want you to fight for us. Fight for the relationship. Realize that the relationship is too valuable to let slip away because of a "mistake" you made. Realize that we are too valuable to lose. When we tell you to stop calling us, we want you to say, "I don't want to lose you, and I will change." We realize you may not care enough to say those words and follow through. But, just putting it out there... when a woman tells you to go away with tears in her eyes, what she's really saying is "If you're going to continue to be a jerk, please don't ever call me again." But what she actually wants is for you to *stop being a jerk*.

> Rob's drunken display, part 1:
> Rob and Laura were juniors at the same college, and had been seeing each other for a couple of months.

They hadn't talked about being exclusive, but neither was dating anyone else. One Friday night, they each had plans with their friends but ended up at the same club. Rob and Laura talked briefly at the club, but each went off to be with his/her friends. Later in the evening, Laura saw Rob on the dance floor all over another woman. Touching her, kissing her, it was quite a drunken display. Through mutual friends Laura was sure he didn't go home with the other woman, that the kissing was the extent of it. Still, it made her feel anything but special. The next day Rob stopped by Laura's as if nothing had happened. When she realized he wasn't apologizing, tears slowly began to fall and she asked him to leave. He asked why, and he was surprised that she cared enough to be upset about him kissing another woman. He respected her wishes, and left. A few weeks went by, and Laura hadn't heard from Rob. He wasn't fighting for her, and it was over. But she wasn't happy, and neither was he. She wanted him to care enough to make things right with her.

Brad's new job:
Brad and Tori were close friends in college but never dated. A couple of years after graduation, while living on opposite coasts, Brad was talking about taking a job near Tori. For a couple of months, he was talking about the opportunities he'd have there and that he looked forward to her being a big part of his life again. Both Brad and Tori were hoping the relationship would be more than a

friendship. When Brad then took a temporary job in another city (nowhere near Tori), he didn't know how to tell her and avoided the issue for a while. They continued to talk often and grow very close. When he finally broke the news, Tori was devastated. And she didn't think it was healthy for her to continue to grow close to him, waiting for him. What would happen when this job is up? Would he choose another job far from her? Was this his way of showing he wasn't interested in a future with her? She told him not to call her anymore. And he didn't. As his temporary position was coming to an end, she reached out to him. She was upset that she hadn't heard from him, and his response was, "You said not to call you!" He was hurt by her decision, but respected it. They were in touch for a little while longer, but the relationship never went anywhere. She wished he had fought for her. If he wanted to continue to grow close to her and plan for the future, he should have fought for it. But he didn't.

In both of the examples above, the guy did something to threaten the security of the relationship. He did something to put distance between them. And as a mature, sane woman, she accepted the change and let go. So if he wants to still be together, he needs to fight for the relationship. He needs to find a way to bring that security back to her. If Rob wanted to continue to date Laura, he could have talked to her about their expectations and found common ground. And although Brad's career move brought him further from Tori, he could have proposed they make definite plans to visit each other, video chat regularly, or some other things to show that he was still invested in her.

When you fight for us and fight for the relationship, it makes us feel special. It makes us feel cared for. And it makes us feel like the relationship is valuable to you, which makes us feel secure.

A Note to the Ladies: If he is the one putting distance between you, he should be the one fighting for the relationship. *You* shouldn't try to find ways to work things out. After telling him how you feel, you need to leave it to him to make the change. And unless he does, you need to just let him go.

22

The wait-and-see

Sometimes after an apology (or in place of one, if the relationship is very new) we get the "wait-and-see." You give us "space" and "time to cool off" before testing the waters again. Then you come back around as if nothing has happened. To us, this is similar to the "I'm sorry" without making amends. Giving us time to cool off really just saves you from having to hear that we're upset. And unless amends are made, it changes nothing.

> Rob's drunken display, part 2:
> When Laura realized that Rob wasn't coming back around to fight for their relationship, she had no choice but to get over it. Weeks went by, and the more she moved on with her life, the more Rob was getting ready to move back in. Because when Laura ended things with Rob after his drunken display, he just took that to mean she needed space. From that day he knew he'd be coming back; he just needed to wait for the right time. About two months after that night, he texted her. "Hey, how have you been?" Having always liked Rob, she was

happy to hear from him and replied. Rob went on to say how he missed her, and that he was sorry. But instead of fighting for her and making things right when he upset her two months ago, he just waited. He hoped she'd somehow forget what happened and want to see him again. Laura asked Rob how she would know that things would be different this time. Rob had no answer. He wasn't prepared to have to win her back. He wasn't prepared to change anything. He just wanted to be the same guy he was, and have her back. Laura missed him, but she was smart enough to realize that this wouldn't work for her. She was sure she'd end up crying again.

Kevin and his emails, part 2:
When Kevin tried to reconnect with Samantha a second time, he didn't write to say, "I'm sorry I lost touch," or make any mention of what happened last time. He just tried to add her as an online friend, as if nothing had happened. Kevin tried the wait-and-see. Samantha, however, was done waiting to hear from him. They haven't been in touch since.

Brett's Olympic trip, part 1:
Linda and Brett had an on-again off-again relationship. They liked each other a lot, but they couldn't seem to get things right. About six months after their last break-up, Brett was happy to hear from Linda again, and they agreed to meet for lunch. Before their date, Linda did a little online reconnaissance. She found some recently posted

pictures of him with another woman whose name was noticeably Greek. Linda figured this was a recent ex-girlfriend, and didn't think much of it. At their lunch date, Brett told Linda he wanted to "take things slowly" with her, and then mentioned in passing that he was going to the Olympics next month. In Athens. "With a friend." It turns out that Brett was still dating the Greek woman, and was going to Athens with her to enjoy the Olympics. They would be staying with her family there. Appalled at how Brett could want to start things up with her again with a trip like this planned, Linda left their date in tears. She gave him an ultimatum. And he chose Athens. Fast-forward six months, and Brett tried to get Linda back. As they were talking things out, Brett actually said, "I thought I could go on the trip with her, and you'd still take me back. Because you love me." To which Linda replied, "You must be out of your freakin' mind."

From our side, the wait-and-see never seems beneficial. If you wanted to make changes for the better, we would have heard from you sooner. If we let you back in after some time has passed, it seems like we'd just be signing ourselves up to be treated poorly again. And as self-respecting, independent women, we think you must be *out of your freakin' mind* to think we'd want that again. Because "I love you" does not mean "You can treat me like crap." Which brings us to the next chapter on the L-word.

23

The L-word

Generally speaking, there seem to be two ways people first use the word "love" in relationships.

There's the "I love you" that means "I love that you are funny and smart, that you get along with my family, that you haven't slept with many people before me, and that you care about making me happy." This kind of love is similar to how we love a material possession. We love what it brings us. This is a selfish kind of love, but not in a bad way. We certainly should choose people who add to our lives.

There's also the "I love you" that means "I care deeply about your feelings, and I would make sacrifices for your happiness." This is a care-taking, generous kind of love. It's the kind of love we might feel for our family members.

And here is the key: For a successful relationship, women and men should feel *both* kinds of love for each other. If we are dating and I've come to care about you very much, but I don't think you're the greatest thing ever, I'm going to feel trapped by my love for you. I won't be happy or fulfilled, but I will find it incredibly difficult to leave. If you think I am the greatest thing ever, but don't show me love and caring, I'm either going to find it elsewhere, or stay with you and cry all the time about how poorly you treat me. But, if we each think the other is the greatest thing, and we are always looking out for each other's feelings, think of how great that relationship would be! No hurt, no crying, lots of fun times, lots of support and friendship. Ideal.

> Brandon was "so in love":
> Mara and Brandon met and started dating toward the end of their junior year of college. Since they hadn't been together long and were both going home for the summer, they didn't think it made much sense to stay together. By the time the fall semester had come around, Brandon met someone else and had fallen "so in love" with her. Although he was "really happy" with his new girlfriend, Brandon was still calling Mara. He would ask her to study together, calling it a date. He would tell Mara how sexy she is, and how he wished he could sleep with her. It was clear to Mara that Brandon's definition of love didn't include caring for his girlfriend's feelings, or even showing respect for her. It was as if Brandon's "I love you" meant, "I love that you're so great to me. I'm going to do whatever I want, but I'm sure you'll still be there because you're so great." A few months later, this new girlfriend "broke his heart" by dumping him. And he cried to Mara about it.

Before you use the L-word, check to see if you feel both kinds of love. If you don't, and you tell her you love her, you will be misleading her. She'll find inconsistencies between your words and your actions. She'll be upset often. And she might even get a little crazy. If you don't yet think she's the greatest woman to walk into your life, or if you don't yet have that deep caring for her, it's better not to use the L-word. You should, however, tell her all the things you love about her and why you love being with her. This is important for us to hear. We can be patient for the deeper feelings, but you should freely articulate the positive feelings you do have for us.

> After six months, Sean had nothing to say:
> Sean and Amanda had been dating for about six months. And over that time, Amanda noticed that Sean never made any mention of his feelings toward her. She didn't need to hear that he loved her, but she did need to hear that he had some positive feelings toward her and their relationship. Because of his past, Sean claimed, it was difficult for him to get excited about being with someone, and he couldn't articulate any positive sentiment toward Amanda. She tried to be sensitive to his experience, but they had been dating for six months already. Surely he should feel enough security to say something like, "It's great that I can truly be myself around you," or "I always have a great time with you." It was a deal breaker for Amanda, and she ended the relationship. A couple of years later (*years!*) Sean got back in touch with Amanda to say how much he missed her. He was finally able to

articulate some feelings, but it was too late. Amanda had moved on.

The deeper feelings will either develop over time (six months or so) or not. Women need to learn to be patient and let this develop. We often want an answer in the first couple of months, but it is too soon for the deep feelings to develop with most men. Ladies, be patient!

And ladies, before you use the L-word to express how much you care, check to see if you also think he's the greatest thing. I know you might think he is in the beginning, but remember that we're all on good behavior for the first couple of months. Before you can decide if he truly is a great guy, you'll need to get to know him pretty well. So, (and how perfect is this) you should also give it about six months to see if you really do think he's the greatest thing.

In short, **stay away from the L-word until you truly <u>know</u> her and <u>care deeply</u> for her.**

And, *this is important*: Guys, once we're in our mid-twenties or older, understand that **we expect love to come with a future**. We're not interested in love for the sake of the experience. We're looking for a love that doesn't leave. So, unless you are both very young, also stay away from the L-word until you're ready to make a commitment. In the meantime, *show her* you love her. If you're tempted to say it because you're oh so in love, but you think you may take a job across the country in a few months, better to just be good to her and show her love. Save the L-word for when you're ready to create a future with her.

24

Hedging your bets

You're excited about the new amazing woman you're dating and it's all going well, yet you're still chatting up other women on the side. You're still going out of your way to get numbers and flirt. Just in case it doesn't work out with your current woman, you'll have a backup waiting in the wings. You are hedging your bets.

Eric's hidden phone:

Jenny and Eric had been dating for about two months, and Eric was very happy to be with her. He often told his friends how great she is, how beautiful she is, and how she laughs at all of his jokes. The first time Eric took a shower at Jenny's place, she was surprised to see him hide his phone before he showered. Jenny wasn't the nosey type and never would have thought to look through his phone. It made her feel horrible to realize that as happy as they were, he must have been at least flirting with other women. She began to wonder whether they really were exclusive, and had a dozen questions ready for him when he got out of the shower. Jenny got jealous and annoying. And the happy relationship ended soon after.

Bill's back burner:
Bill and Lila became very close friends at work, but the timing was just never right for them to date. Fast forward a few years, Bill and Lila no longer worked together or lived in the same town. Every now and then, Bill would contact Lila and talk about wanting to date her and about wanting a future with her. But nothing ever seemed to work out. The vacations, the trips to visit, and the long phone dates never happened. He never seemed to choose her. And later, she found out why. For most of the time they were in touch, he had a girlfriend. Lila felt completely misled, and didn't even want to keep a friendship with Bill. He was keeping her on the back burner, just in case his current relationship didn't work out.

Hedging will always backfire. We'll be able to sense that you are paying attention to another woman, and it will keep us from feeling secure. You'll be hiding your phone, not taking calls or checking email in front of us. We'll know something is up. And (here is the kicker), we do not enjoy the competition. We just don't. Mature, sensible women do not fight for men. Maybe if the situation was reversed, you'd be fueled to work harder for us, to "win" us. But it's not true for women. We will cry our eyes out, leave, and hate you forever. Or we'll stay, but not trust you and get jealous and annoying. Either way, you will ruin every good relationship this way. You will also lose every (sane, drama-free) woman on your list. Every last one. No woman wants to be on the back burner while you're dating someone else. We don't want to be your second choice. That doesn't make us feel special at all.

If the woman you're currently dating is a great catch and you're telling your friends how happy you are, you need to respect her and respect the relationship. Care for her, and make her feel special and secure. You don't have to commit to marrying her, but you have to show her some care. After all, you've been practicing your skills with the ladies for a while now, Romeo. If things don't work out in this relationship, it won't take long for you to find another. So live in the present. Give your relationship the chance to be the fun, happy companionship you're looking for. And quit hedging your bets.

A Note to the Ladies: Again I have to suggest that you do not go fishing for information. Do not look through his phone. Do not read his emails. You will undoubtedly find something to misunderstand. You'll make things up in your head about it, and you will ruin the relationship. If you have no reason to think he's playing around, be happy! And continue to give him his privacy.

25

The hit and run

You're trying to figure out your plans for the weekend, and it seems you can fit everything in if you stop by her place on your way out with the guys on Friday night. The hit and run. Lovely.

No woman wants to be the victim of a hit and run. Either she is your plan for the night, or she is not. She is not going to be your pre-party or your after-party. Remember that we are looking to feel special. Fitting us in on your way out or coming to our place after a night out with the boys is not our idea of special.

We understand, you had a tough week. It's your buddy's birthday and you have to go out tonight. And you really, *really* need to let off some steam so you can enjoy your weekend. We totally understand, and honestly we'd prefer that you're not horny when you go out with the guys. But we are not going to make this acceptable. You'll get all the quickies and sleepovers you want when you *marry* the girl. Until then, give her all the love she deserves when you can offer her your full attention.

A Note to the Ladies: Women, work with me here. Stand up for what you deserve, and do not let him talk you into coming over. Not before his night out, and not at 3AM as he leaves the club. If you make this acceptable, it will become the norm. You won't have real dates, you won't feel special, and you'll become the annoying girlfriend.

26

Respect

It doesn't matter if you are the best athlete in the world, earn $100 million a year, or have been voted the World's Sexiest Man. Being powerful does not mean the rules are different for you. It does not entitle you to lie, cheat, or otherwise disrespect your woman. We are all human beings.

Perhaps you want to be the breadwinner, and have a woman who doesn't work outside the home. That's perfectly fine. But you do not get to treat her like she is any less than you. Not while you are dating, and not after you marry. She is not your servant, your personal chef, or your housekeeper. She is your partner. If you choose to divide the work in a way that puts you in the office and her in the home, that's fine. But she is still your partner, and you have to respect her. You have to respect the work she does and her role in the relationship.

Or perhaps you want a woman who matches your intellect, your athleticism, and your success in business. That's also perfectly fine. But if she falls short of your high expectations, you still have to treat her with respect. You can choose not to be with her, but you still have to be respectful to her.

And in general, regardless of any predefined relationship roles, you have to be considerate of her feelings. If you can't, you shouldn't be in the relationship.

> Brett's Olympic trip, part 2:
> Remember Brett who thought Linda would take him back after he went to Athens for the Olympics with another woman? When he admitted this to Linda, she couldn't help but feel like he thought of her as a lesser being. Brett knew he wanted to ultimately be with Linda, yet thought it acceptable to make her cry for days and wait months for him while he had the once in a lifetime experience of going to the Olympics and while he spent quality time with another woman's family. Linda certainly didn't feel cared for, and with good reason. Brett cared only about what he would gain from it all.

> Jason's dirty uniform:
> Jason and Cara were in their early twenties and had been dating for a few years. They often talked about marriage, but it would be after she finished law school and after he advanced some in his career. For now, he was still living at home and she had an apartment near school. On the weekends, Jason played football in her neighborhood. After his game, he'd shower at her place and they'd spend the day together. On one of these days, his uniform

was particularly dirty. And after his shower, there was quite a bit of dirt left in the bathroom. When Cara saw this, she said, "Jason, I think you left something in the bathroom." He looked in and said, "What did I leave? I don't see anything." "How about all that dirt?" Jason rolled his eyes and made some careless attempt to clean it. When Cara later noticed the dirt still left in the bathroom and said something to Jason, he said, "It's your job to clean it!" Well, Cara let him have it. "Listen, I don't know what your mother does for you at home, but I am not your maid. This is my apartment and you need to clean up after yourself here." Even if Jason innocently misunderstood their roles at first (and that's a big "if"), when she first mentioned the problem he should have respected her wishes and handled it completely. This would have shown that Jason cared about Cara's happiness.

Remember, you chose to be with her. If you can't respect her, you won't be making her feel special, cared for, or secure. So, if you can't respect her, you should get out of the relationship.

27

Toughening up
Miss Sensitive

You're dating this great woman, and you often have a great
time together. But sometimes she's sensitive. Too
sensitive. She gets upset if you tease her, she gets upset if
she thinks you're paying attention to another woman, and
she gets upset if you don't call her when you say you will.
She needs to toughen up.

So you continue to tease her, pay attention to other
women, and not call when you say you will. But strangely,
she isn't getting any better with it. In fact, the situation is
getting worse. Let me explain.

**The only way we become less sensitive is by becoming
more secure.**

If you want to tease her, you first have to make her 100%
sure that you love her exactly as she is. If you want to be
able to chat with another woman at a bar without it being a
problem, you have to first make sure your woman knows

you only want to be with her. Make sure she knows how much you enjoy her company, and that you'd never do anything to mess up your relationship with her. And if you want the freedom to be able to miss a phone call every now and then, you first have to make sure she knows you're still thinking of her and will call soon after.

> Jim's perfect ring, part 2:
> The first time Annie was at Jim's apartment (the day he told her about the "perfect ring" he designed for his ex-fiancée), she noticed a stack of mail on the coffee table with another woman's name on it. The mail was to Jim's ex who hadn't lived there in over six months, and he was collecting it for her. He'd mail her a package every couple of weeks, or call if something looked important. When Annie told Jim that she didn't feel good about this, he dismissed her feelings and chose not to do anything differently. When it came up again (because nothing had changed, of course it would come up again!) he said that she needed to toughen up. He no longer had feelings for the ex, and that should be enough for Annie to let it go. If everything else in the relationship had been going well, this one thing might not have been a big deal to Annie. But given that he was still talking about the perfect ring he made for the same ex, Annie was wondering if this woman wasn't just in his past. She was feeling very insecure about his past relationship, and Jim's attempt to toughen Annie up had backfired.

28

Testing, testing...

One thing that continues to boggle my logical mind is why men would test us, why they would create for us a difficult situation just to see how we would handle it.

Maybe you want to be sure not to date a woman who gets needy, for example. So you purposely test her to see if she gets needy. You think she's great, you always have a good time together, and you would never normally wait three days to call her. But, after the first time you sleep with her, you test her by waiting three days before calling.

Essentially you are saying, "If I decide to pull back from her, let's see how she'll react." But all she sees is that you're pulling back. You don't have any intention on being the guy who waits three days to call, because you want to talk to her all the time. But she doesn't know that anymore. She doesn't know it's just a test, and now you're Mr. Inconsistent. So she doesn't feel secure, and she'll get annoying, jealous, maybe even crazy. But, everything was fine before. You created this.

Or maybe you can't deal with a jealous girlfriend, so you test your new woman by purposely flirting with other women in her presence, or by getting together with an ex "just for lunch." You have no desire to see your ex for lunch or to mess things up with your new woman, but you want to be sure she won't get jealous. All she sees, however, is that you've changed. You're inconsistent, and she's now insecure, which means you'll both be unhappy.

When you test us, you are designing your behavior to be inconsistent with what we know about you. You are introducing something unnatural into the relationship, and you are judging us based on our reaction to it. It just doesn't make sense.

To see if we'll become needy or jealous, or to see if we'll develop any other undesirable trait, you'll have to wait until a situation arises naturally. Just be your normal self, and see how we react. (Same advice to the ladies, of course!)

By testing us, you are setting us up to fail. When you test us, you are creating unnatural obstacles in the relationship. **You can't create obstacles for the relationship and expect the relationship to go well.** You just can't.

29

Your crazy ex-girlfriends

They seemed normal when you started to date them. They seemed emotionally stable. They seemed totally cool. Then they lost it. They cheated and blamed you, they contacted the ex-girlfriend you were in love with, they keyed your new car. What happened? Finally, you thought, you found a normal one. She has good, normal friends. She comes from a functioning family. But one day, she just flipped out.

If you have at least one crazy ex-girlfriend, you might want to take a look at the messages you were sending. **Inconsistent messages will make her crazy.** Like flipping a switch.

We understand you're not perfect. We understand sometimes it takes time to figure out what you want or what works for you, and that sometimes it's just not us. That's fine. But when there are inconsistencies between what you say and what you do, when you change your mind (seemingly) overnight, and when you move on incredibly quickly, how are we supposed to deal? We are looking for security and you have been doing your best to give that to us. Then, in a matter of minutes, it is all gone. Can you blame us for not knowing how to deal with the sudden loss, with the rollercoaster ride, or with all the mixed messages floating around in our heads? Sure, ideally we'd all be able to handle every single thing life throws at us. But until a woman has been through it at least once, she won't know how to cope. If she's been on the rollercoaster before, she'll recognize it and change her expectations. If she's been loved and left in an instant, she'll know what to do to move forward. But the first time around, or even the first time with you, inconsistencies can really just make her crazy. Because if she truly does love you, and your feelings seem to have taken a 180° turn, it is probably the hardest thing she's ever had to deal with in her life. And she just doesn't know how.

Why did she act crazy?

> Maybe because they were talking about living together, even picked out an apartment. Then he suddenly decided to take a job 300 miles away. Something about a "fresh start."

> Maybe because he told her how much he cared about her, but that he had to date someone his mother would approve of. And when he started dating this new woman, he was still calling the ex, hoping to have phone sex with her. Maybe that was it.

> Maybe it was the "hello" e-card he sent her on Valentine's Day just a month after breaking up with

her. An e-card, on *Valentine's Day*, just to say hello.
Seriously?

Maybe it was how over the course of an hour they
were planning their future together and then
breaking up. Some kind of epiphany he had after
hearing something on TV. Could it have been that?
Maybe. But if that didn't do it, seeing that he went
back to online dating the very next morning
probably made her crazy. Yeah, that was probably
it!

We know you're not perfect, but if this is the best you can
do, you should be prepared for our reactions. These may
include:

Calling you every hour, on the hour, until you
F***ING PICK UP THE PHONE!!!!!

Leaving you an incredibly emotional message each
time you don't pick up, including, but not limited to,
bouts of crying hysteria.

Between phone calls, texting you to ask why you
aren't taking our calls. (Yes, we are delusional at
this point. Any sane person would know you're not
ever going to take another one of our calls. But you
flipped the crazy switch on us. So asking why you
won't talk to us is now a perfectly logical question.)

Driving to your house to talk to you because you
wouldn't PICK UP THE F***ING PHONE!!!!!!!!!!!!!

Or perhaps:

> Calling your best friend, your mom, and your sister to help us understand what just happened. (Joke's on us when they say, "Yeah, that sounds like him.")

> Coming to see you at work, knowing you wouldn't create a scene there. But then crying, creating the scene ourselves.

How to avoid the crazy:

> First things first. If you know you have some intimacy or commitment issues, deal with them before you get close to us. Talk to your mom, your priest, a therapist, whoever. Just talk it out before it affects us. Or at least be fully aware of the limitations you have and make them clear to us.

> Don't talk about "our future," "our kids," or "our life together" until you are ready to put a ring on our finger. *Seriously.* That sort of talk messes us up in the head. When you say those words, we believe them. We believe you want a future, kids, and a life with us. We envision it, and we start to feel secure. Then later on when you realize you don't want all that with us, we're devastated.

> Avoid the sudden extremes. "We should talk about moving in together." Then a week later, "I don't think I ever want to get married or live with anyone." Perhaps you can understand how this could make a woman crazy.

Be honest with yourself and us about what you want. If you are sure we are dating to find "the one," and you know we are not the one for you or that you are not ready to find her, don't lead us on.

You already know how to keep things from getting crazy in other situations. In dealing with people at work, for example, you'd be consistent with how you treated them. You wouldn't change things day to day because of how you felt in the moment. You'd think things through and make smooth transitions. This would keep the relationships at their best and earn you respect. The same care should be offered to the women you date.

A Note to the Ladies: You must learn to recognize the inconsistencies so you can get out before you act crazy. As soon as you notice him being inconsistent, talk to him about it. If he is receptive to your comments and pays more attention to the issue, that's great. If he gets defensive, however, get yourself out of that relationship and save yourselves the drama.

30
Break-ups

Break-ups are never easy. But there are ways to minimize the hurt and drama. If you want to break up with us, the best way is to say that you have thought a lot about it, and you are sure this is not what you want.

Do not confuse us by saying how much you love us and how difficult it is to break up. Our response will be, "Are you sure this is what you want? Maybe you are just scared. We can work this out." Then you'll agree to try to work on it, and you'll break up with us again the next week. In the meantime, we've gotten our hopes back up, and we'll fall twice as hard when you finally do leave.

Do not end the relationship with goodbye sex. We won't see it as goodbye sex; we'll see it as getting-him-back sex. I mean, how could you possibly want to break up with us after we just had the most incredible time in bed? We're connected! It's much more than physical! We are one! Yes, break-up sex will do that to us. If we were at all attached to you or the idea of having you, we will not be able to let go after break-up sex.

Do give us reasons, if we ask. If you realize we don't want the same things, explain that to us. If, after getting to know us, you realize we're not what you are looking for, explain that to us (if we ask). The more logical the argument, the easier it will be for us to accept.

Do own your part. If you led us on, admit it. Otherwise we will still believe everything you said to us about wanting to be with us. We will be completely confused, and we will want answers.

If there is someone else, be very careful about telling us this. It could be the best or worst thing you say. No self-respecting woman would want to be with a guy who chooses someone else over her. So if you break up and cite "someone else" as your reason, this could make for the quickest, easiest break-up you ever had. However, if she has recently exhibited any crazy behavior, the less information you give her the better. If she's not thinking clearly and you tell her you are interested in someone else, she'll likely become your super-sleuth ex and try to identify the woman. She'll read all the posts on your Facebook page. Yes, *all* of them, repeatedly clicking the "Older Posts" link until she finds that you "joined Facebook." She'll click on all the pages of all the cute girls who are in your friend list, and if she can't see their pages she'll have her friends who *can* see their pages log in. She'll figure it out. Then she'll call you at random times in tears, wanting to know why you choose the new woman over her. (As if the fact that she calls you in tears doesn't make that obvious.) But that's all *only* if she's recently acted a little crazy. If not, she'll probably tear up your pictures, but that's about it.

And after you break up with us, especially if you're interested in someone else, please do not try to be friends with us. If you propose we stay in touch as friends, and we agree, it's because we want to leave the door open to getting you back. But you don't want us. So don't do that to us. Go away peacefully. Wish us well and let us move on.

A Note to the Ladies: After he has broken up with you, be honest with yourself about why you want to stay in touch. If you are just trying to leave the door open to getting back together, you're just setting yourself up for a harder fall. He broke up with you. Let him go.

31

Holiday and birthday presents

Let me start this chapter by saying that I whole-heartedly believe it is the thought that counts. So when you give us a cookbook as a holiday present, exactly what thought are you trying to convey?

Unless we specifically ask for it, presents **should not be anything domestic**. Ever. We know some guys love to get expensive tools, but how much would you like it if you didn't ask for it? Then it's the gift that you know will come with a chore list. It's the same for us with kitchen appliances, house wares, cookbooks, etc.

> Matt's cookbook present:
> Sofia dated Matt while they were young, teens into twenties. As they got older, Matt recognized that his brother's wife often prepared nice parties including lots of stylish appetizers. So as one of her Christmas presents, he bought Sofia a fancy cookbook. While the present itself was

appreciated, Sofia understood that he wanted her to cook for him more often. And quite frankly, she thought he should learn to cook the stylish appetizers himself.

It wasn't as if Matt and Sofia often cooked romantic dinners together and it would be something to bring them closer. Essentially, Matt was giving Sofia a self-help book. As a holiday gift.

Holiday and birthday gifts **should not be lingerie** (unless maybe for Valentine's Day, more on that below). Don't get me wrong; we do think sex is an important part of a healthy relationship. And as the relationship grows, the sexual part of the relationship will grow as well. Most women would be happy to sport some sexy new underthings, but since this is just as much a present for you as it is for her, these should not take the place of a holiday or birthday present.

When you're giving her something for the holidays or her birthday, it **should be something you know she wants or you know she would appreciate**. If she has been searching all over town for her favorite perfume, and you found it when you went to visit your brother in Boston, that's a great present. It shows you pay attention to what makes her happy. It shows that you care. If you know she's been stressed out from work lately but she can't spend the money on a nice massage, a spa gift card would be a great present. Or even a more economical and intimate version would be for you to read up on how to give a good massage, buy some massage oil and serene music, and make a romantic night of it. (Make sure you do, however, give her the full massage. This is a gift for her.)

> Gary's birthday gift for Lynn:
> While walking through the bookstore one day, Lynn mentioned to Gary that she'd love to get this very expensive language software and refresh her French. Although Gary was still in grad school and couldn't afford to buy the expensive software, he asked everyone he knew if they had a copy. Sure enough, just in time for her birthday, he was able to borrow the software and install it on her computer. He bought a couple of things for her too, but this present meant just as much to Lynn as anything he paid for. This took time and effort, and showed that he was listening. It showed that he cared about her happiness.

Valentine's Day presents

If you already have a pretty active sex life, sure, lingerie is a great part of her Valentine's Day present. You might want to supplement it with some chocolates, wine, or something else you know she would enjoy. If you just started having sex, I'd stay away from the lingerie and let that develop in its own time. Go for perfume or fancy chocolates instead. Flowers are also great on Valentine's day, but not if they're the same flowers you're giving your mom.

Eddie's big balloons:
Eddie and Kristen went to college together and had been dating for a couple of years. They both lived on campus but were heading back to visit Eddie's family for the weekend to celebrate his dad's 50th birthday. It happened to be Valentine's Day weekend, so when Eddie arrived to pick Kristen up, he brought her a gift. It was the newest, trendiest Valentine's gift, flowers inside a balloon. It was all the craze at the mall. And Kristen loved it. The balloon was clear with white flowers printed on it, and inside were red roses. But when Kristen got into Eddie's car for their trip, she was confused. There was another balloon with flowers in the back seat. "I bought that one for my mom," Eddie said. And his mom's balloon had "I love you" printed on it. "But her flowers are carnations! Yours are roses! I gave you the roses!" Now, one could argue that roses are better than carnations, or that an "I love you" balloon is better than one without, and one could always argue that mom trumps girlfriend. But the point of the story is that there would be no arguing had Eddie not given the same present to his girlfriend and mom. It was a nice present, but it didn't make Kristen feel special.

Unfortunately, this wasn't Eddie's only Valentine's Day fumble.

Eddie's lingerie model:
A couple of years later, Eddie was living back home after college. It was just before Valentine's Day and

Eddie's mom was taking his sister and her friend to the outlet mall. Eddie joined them so he could buy a Valentine's Day gift for Kristen. After splitting with the mom (supposedly), the rest of the group headed over to the lingerie store. As if it wasn't bad enough that Eddie's mom would know he was buying Kristen lingerie, Eddie didn't know Kristen's bra size. So he said to his sister's friend, "Kristen is about your size. What size do you wear?" Not only did Eddie buy lingerie in the other girl's size, he asked her to try it on! *And it was completely sheer!* Kristen was upset for weeks about this. And, of course, she made her own trip to the outlet mall to exchange the lingerie for the biggest, boxiest pajamas she could find.

Gifts for other women

It's worth mentioning here that gifts for female friends other than your girlfriend should never be jewelry or anything romantic.

Alex chose earrings:
Alex was enjoying his first real job after finishing his graduate business degree. He was working for a large company and became friendly with one of his more senior colleagues. She was 35 and single, with an 8-year-old son. Alex was 26 and was dating Lana, 24. When the holidays came around, Alex wanted to buy something for this woman at work.

131

Instead of something office related (or sports related, or related to any other interest she might have), Alex chose to get her a pair of gold earrings. Well, Lana was less than pleased with his choice and was sure he had some sort of crush on this woman. Alex's choice made Lana feel anything but special. And this woman at work became an issue in their relationship.

Remember that you want your girlfriend to feel cared for, so get her something you know will make her happy. And remember that you want her to always feel special, so don't get the same thing for someone else, or something romantic for another woman.

32

Know your history

Please Note: I am not a physician, and it is not the intention of this book to provide specific medical advice. Please consult with a qualified physician for diagnosis and for answers to your personal questions.

This is a sensitive topic for many single women. We're excited to be in a great new relationship with a great new guy. We're monogamous, and before ditching the condoms we both get tested for STDs. We're all clear, and everything's great. Then, months later, we get our regular pap test. We've tested positive for HPV. And we're furious. You didn't know you carried it. But, should you have known?

Well, for most people there aren't any signs or symptoms. But you should have had the STD talk with all of your exes, even if you always used a condom. And if any of your exes has ever had a bout with HPV, there is a chance you carry it.

So, yes, you should have known. Or at least you should have known that it was possible.

Some strains of HPV can cause cervical cancer. *Cancer.* HPV can also contribute to difficulties carrying a pregnancy to term. And it needs to be our choice to take that risk with our bodies. You owe us that information. So before we have sex, you have to let us know your history.

Even if we never have anything more than an abnormal pap test, you can bet that we will be upset to find out you haven't had this discussion with your exes, or that you didn't mention anything to us. We won't feel cared for. And since this can be a serious issue, it will likely have a significant impact on the relationship.

So if you are going to sleep with a woman, it is your responsibility to **know your history**. No excuses.

33
Gratitude

This is probably the most important chapter in this book.

If you are not the type of person who is grateful every day for what you have, I honestly don't think you'll ever be in a lasting, happy relationship. And the reason is this: You can always find a reason to break up with someone. People aren't perfect. And no two are a perfect match. To have a happy, successful, lasting relationship, you have to focus on what's good.

Staying in a relationship is a choice we make every day. If you don't wake up every day grateful for having this person in your life, you won't be treating her well. And either she'll leave, or she'll be miserable. Of course, the same holds true for women. She can't expect you to stay or to be happy if she's not grateful for you each day, as well.

> Jesse graduated to gratitude:
> Jesse and Liz started dating while away at different colleges. Although Jesse told Liz he wouldn't date anyone else, he did in fact date other women on

campus. On one of her visits to Jesse's campus, Liz found out about another woman. And for the rest of their college careers, there was a cycle of breaking up, getting back together, and Jesse cheating again. After college they decided to give it another try, and something clicked for Jesse. He started to feel grateful for having Liz in his life. He thought about what he wanted for his future, and he felt lucky to have her. Jesse began to treat Liz better than he ever had. Since then, they have been very happy.

Kelly learned to appreciate her artist:
Kelly and Nick dated for about 8 years before they moved to Los Angeles. Kelly was a teacher, and Nick was an artist. As she thought about her future, Kelly wondered if Nick would ever have a stable income, and wondered if Nick truly was the guy for her. She had grown comfortable with him, but no longer felt passionate about her struggling artist boyfriend. She decided to see what else was out there in LA, and ended their relationship. She was excited that she might find passion again, and that she might find a man with a more secure career. Kelly went on a several dates over the course of a few months, and was terribly disappointed. She recognized many things about Nick that were important to her. Most of all, she missed his companionship every day. When she told him how she felt, he was happy to have her back. She now wakes up grateful every day for having him in her life. She focuses on what he brings to the

relationship rather than what he might lack. They have been very happy together since.

I truly believe gratitude is the key to being happy in general. If you aren't grateful every day for what you have, you can't know true happiness. Life is hard, and not everything that comes our way brings us joy. If we choose to focus on the hardships and sadness, we're in for one long and miserable life! Every day we must choose to find happiness. See it when it is in front of you. Look for it within what you have. And every day that we choose to stay in a relationship, we have to recognize the good it brings to our lives. We have to be grateful for what we have.

34

Fake it 'til you make it

Throughout this book I've been saying that women want to feel special, cared for, and secure, even from the very beginning of the relationship. But you're not going to know on day one if we're someone worth caring for, if we'll truly be special to you, or if you'll want to pursue a lasting relationship with us.

The best way to figure this out is to treat her like she's special, treat her like you care, and be consistent so she feels secure. I'm not saying you should mislead her; I'm saying that until you have an opinion, act as if she's special. Act as if you care. Because the worst thing you can do in the beginning of a relationship is treat her poorly. Nothing good can ever come from a poor start.

Eventually you will know if she is worth your time and your efforts. You'll know if she is special to you and if you truly care. And if she's not the one for you, there's never any shame in being a great guy.

Situations where you should fake it 'til you make it:

> *Asking "How was your day?"* You might not care about every detail she mentions, but you'll get to know a lot about her with this one question.
>
> *Hanging out with her friends.* Eventually you'll either find common interests and you'll like hanging out with them, or you won't. But to figure that out you'll have to be open to having a good time with them.
>
> *Trusting her.* Until you have any reason not to, you have to trust her. So your last two girlfriends cheated and you are having a hard time with trust. Fake it. Eventually you will have enough reason to trust her (or not). But in the beginning, you certainly don't want to ruin things because of your past. Check that baggage and enjoy the flight, until you have reason to feel otherwise.
>
> *Gratitude.* You want to have a good relationship, and you want to focus on the positive. But you're not sure how to get into that habit. It's simple: Say to yourself, "I am grateful for having her in my life." "I am grateful for my good health." "I am grateful that I have a decent job." Say it. Even if you're not feeling grateful. Just say it. Keep saying it. Eventually you'll feel it.

You should fake it 'til you make it in situations where you don't yet have an opinion, situations you are willing to explore.

Situations where you should *not* fake it:

> *In bed.* There shall be no faking anything in bed. Both partners must be able to feel open and honest with all things naked. Gentle guidance is appropriate. Faking it is not.

> *Any situation involving lying.* Lying is never appropriate.

Final words

So go ahead, get started:

> Ask her how her day was.
> Call when you say you'll call.
> Pick up her favorite bottle of wine.
> Create new memories with her.
> Tell her what you like about her.
> If you make a mistake, make proper amends.
> Be open and honest with her.
> Focus on one woman at a time.
> Make proper dates, scheduled in advance.
> Recognize and respect what she brings to the relationship.
> Be consistent.
> Be grateful.

And enjoy the time you spend together.

I hope you've found some useful insight here. And if nothing else, I hope the topics here have initiated dialogue in your relationship so you can determine what works best for you.

Thank you for reading.

Rebecca

CPSIA information can be obtained
at www.ICGtesting.com
Printed in the USA
LVOW01s0845270417
532393LV00016B/362/P